STONE THROWERS

by

Kelvin L. Thomas Ministries

ksonrise.09@gmail.com

kelvinthomasministries.com

Design
Sylvia Thomas

Photography
Sykari Thomas

To Throw the Stone

Jesus went across to Mount Olives,
but he was soon back in the Temple
again. Swarms of people came to him.
He sat down and taught them.
The religion scholars and Pharisees
led in a woman who had been caught
in an act of adultery. They stood her
in plain sight of everyone and said,
"Teacher, this woman was caught
red-handed in the act of adultery.
Moses, in the Law, gives orders to
stone such persons. What do you
say?" They were trying to trap him
into saying something incriminating
so they could bring charges against
him.
Jesus bent down and wrote with his
finger in the dirt. They kept at him,

badgering him. He straightened up and said, "The sinless one among you, go first: Throw the stone." Bending down again, he wrote some more in the dirt.

Hearing that, they walked away, one after another, beginning with the oldest. The woman was left alone. Jesus stood up and spoke to her. "Woman, where are they? Does no one condemn you?"

"No one, Master."

"Neither do I," said Jesus. "Go on your way. From now on, don't sin." -John 8:2-11

Acknowledgement

I thank God, my Heavenly Father for His ever-present help! For it is in Him, that we live, move and have our being. Thank You God!

I want to thank my mother in-law, Annie Rose Harris, for the wonderful write up in "Forwarding" this book. After 37 years of marriage to her baby girl, I would say she has gotten to know me pretty well through the highs and lows of life.

I give honor to Sylvia, my wife, who carries the load while I work, study, pray, meditate and write. She is also my primary editor and cover designer. She is gifted and anointed in this way! Thank you to my daughter Tena D. and my baby girl Sykari. My love, appreciation and admiration for you grow more each day. To my only begotten son, Koric, thank you for your help and sharing your spiritual nuggets of wisdom with me. It is not always easy to digest, but each is worth chewing on.

I want to give a shout of thanks to my eight siblings, who are very supportive of me and has helped to pull out the best of me. I am making it a point to list each by name to show the world how blessed I am.

Robert (Bobby), Bishop Marvin, Millicent, Kenneth, Cedric, Kenneth, Crystal and Millicent.

Yes, what you see is correct, I have two sisters' named Millicent and two Brothers' named Kenneth. I am little brother, middle brother and big brother all at the same time. I am truly blessed. Thanks to each of you and I love you to life!

Thank you to other family members and close friends. God has encircled me with your love and support; for this I am grateful to you. Blessings to you!!!

Mrs. Minnie Thomas Brown
1932 - 2014

A "special corner" for a special lady, my mom,
Minnie Thomas Brown (MTB).

I am eternally grateful. Your vision of the possibilities and your drive and determination to give each of us an opportunity to reach our goals is unparalleled.

Thank You Mom!

Preface

This book is about the goodness of God and the Grace of God, and God's mercy toward all. In my daily prayer, I simply ask God for "health, wealth and wisdom." I pray this with my whole mind for my household (my family). I give thanks to God at all time. I receive this promise, I believe it, and I live with expectations of the blessings happening in my life in Jesus Name. I truly believe this simple prayer mixed with faith has blessed me and my family beyond measure. Even with all of the blessings it does not mean we are exempt from the troubles and trials of this world. In fact, I am praying my way through a situation even as I write this book. But God blesses me with the wisdom to deal with it and grow through it. For this I am grateful!

I want to be transparent in my writing and not just throw scriptures at you, but I also want to share my life struggles and triumphs with you. I always had the desire to write but never thought I developed the skills to be a writer. A couple of years ago I told my son I wanted to write a book and he reminded me of all the writings, notes and messages to him and his sister most of their lives, even into adulthood. "Dad, you have your little messages all over the place and written on anything you can find to write on? I would not be surprised if you wrote a book," he said to me. That for me was revelation, knowledge, wisdom and confirmation that I can and should write my messages (books) for the world to see and to glorify God. The writing of these books also reaffirms in me that, "I Can Do All Things Through Christ Who Strengthens Me."

I no longer say that I am not a writer. This is the third book I have been blessed by the Holy Spirit to pen. "<u>Power Crumbs</u>", "<u>Arise</u>", and now, "<u>Stone Throwers</u>". In saying this, I also have to give thanks to Sylvia, my wife. She is the one who can interpret my writings. She tells me that I write the way I speak. I realized later on that it was not really a compliment after watching her make all the corrections from my numerous drafts. To God be the glory!

Please note that at close of each chapter I speak blessings right into the atmosphere by stating, "Blessings to You." I believe we have the God given power and authority to shift the atmosphere and command the blessings, through the power of our words.

"Faithfulness is what you do, but loyalty is who you are. Who you are always has to outshine what you do, because what you do can be tainted with the wrong motives."
-Kimberly Daniels, Clean House, Strong House

IT IS ALWAYS A GOOD TIME TO PRAY!

Father in Heaven, we give thanks and honor to you. We thank you for your love and kindness, your grace and your mercy. We thank you for giving us a sound mind. The kind of mind that is focused on you and the kingdom work you have for us to do.

We pray that your mighty winds of change, peace, love, and forgiveness will blow through our nation, this world and through each one of us individually. We will follow the pattern and the plans that you have scripted in your Word. Let us not harden our hearts. Speak to us now that we would open our hearts, listen with our spiritual ear to hear what the Holy Spirit is saying to us. Move us swiftly in the direction guided by the blowing winds of your spirit.

Father teach us how to love each other in spite of our differences. Show us how to forgive each other and care for each other. Heavenly Father, when the stones of life are thrown at us, do not let these stones become stumbling blocks but rather turn them into stepping stones to reach the greater levels of love in this life that you called us to.

We acknowledge you in all our ways as you have promised to direct our path. We humble ourselves in the presence of all mankind, because you are God and God alone. There is pure joy in our hearts for you this day. You have the power to do to us and to do through us, things we cannot do for ourselves. We trust that your plan is to prosper us and not to harm us but to give us hope and a greater future.

Bless us God and please do it right now. You can do greater things through us. We believe in you Lord and we put our trust in you. We receive these blessings in the Name of Jesus, Amen.

TABLE OF CONTENT

Chapter One

STONE THROWERS

The impact caused by rock throwing or rock slinging can be hurtful, dangerous and even cause death. Growing up I did not have close access to recreation centers, ball fields or gymnasiums. My siblings, friends and I created a lot of outside games such as, jumping across ditches, rolling truck tires, track races in the street and rock battles. In these rock battles we would normally have teams on each side to gather large rocks to throw at each other. The intent was to hide behind the houses and throw the rock to hit but not to hurt anyone on the other team. I was fortunate enough to have four brothers. The five of us created quite a challenge for most of the neighboring teams. In that we were adolescents, we never contemplated the possibility of breaking a window, denting the side of a house or hitting an occasional car. One day during one of our rock battles I took the chance to peep around the corner of the house and was hit by a rock just above my right eyelid, piercing the skin and causing blood to spew out all over my face. Immediately the battle was over as both teams were shocked at how bad we could hurt each other just from throwing rocks. After this incident there were no more rock battles in our neighborhood. We all learned a valuable lesson of how dangerous throwing rocks could be. Thank God my eye was not lost in the battle and I fully recovered. There is a small scar above my eye as a reminder of the damage done from a not well thought out game.

Like my childhood rock throwing battle, we do not have a full grasp of the impact or the damage we can cause by throwing stones (hurtful words or actions) at other people. These hurtful stones can negatively alter the path of people's lives, leaving them scarred for life and possibly causing death in their careers, death in relationships, mental death or even death of life. So be careful of the stones you throw! If stones are thrown at you, do not throw them back, instead use them as building blocks to help build a stronger character in self and a better foundation for your life. Scripture tells us to resist the devil and he will flee from you. We must pray and ask God for the strength to resist negative temptations. We should ask for spiritual discernment to recognize the attacks of the enemy and receive the grace to grow without causing hurt.

According to Wikipedia - A lithobolos or stone thrower is an artillery weapon that was used in ancient warfare and medieval warfare. But there are a couple of simpler definitions of stone throwers I found in an Urban dictionary that is a more fitting as reference for this book. The definition of "stone throwers" is defined as one who blames others for their own faults, even to the point of falsely accusing and throwing hurtful words or actions (rocks) at another person. This happens to people more often than I would like to mention. When you are falsely accused it will hurt and hurt deeply, especially when it comes from someone closest to you. You do not have to hold on to the hurt. You can simply let it go! When you let it go, trust God to give you the supernatural ability to release the hurt and to release the person who hurt you.

> *A stone thrower is one who acts without thinking about the consequences that one's action might have on others; one who blames others for the fault which they have themselves. This is a form of "Spiritual Warfare."*

I believe that the greatest gift ever given, is the gift of forgiveness! God "gave" His only son to die on the cross for us all. We trade our sinfulness for Jesus's sinlessness! "God demonstrated His own love towards us, while we were still throwing stones (sinners), Christ died for us". This limitless depth of forgiveness played out as a model of how we are to forgive others. If our sins could be measured from least to highest, I believe unforgiveness would be the highest. We unnecessarily carry this heavy burden of unforgiveness around like big dump trucks; fully loaded with no dumping grounds. We are not built for such a heavy load! It is not in God's plans for us to carry the burden of unforgiveness.

Give your burdens to the LORD, and he will take care of you. He will not permit the godly to slip and fall. Psalms 55:22 (NLT)

For so many self-centered reasons, we hold onto the junk that weigh us down.

6

We prefer to wallow in misery, self-inflicted pain because of our unwillingness to forgive. We take the low road and accept the role of being the victim, when God has purposed us to be the victors. When this happens, we have to not allow that "whoa with me" attitude to creep in. Seeing oneself as the victim weakens the internal power to release and let things go. The power of forgiveness is in you. This is a gift from God to man!

There is a very familiar story in the Bible where Jesus demonstrates the power of forgiveness and conviction of the hearts of self-righteous accusers, who I refer to as stone throwers. Although I have read this story and heard the story of casting the first stone many times, in this season of my life I am inspired to give witness to the power of forgiveness. This book, "Stone Throwers" is taken from the bible story of a woman guilty of committing adultery; caught in the very act, yet escaped being stoned to death.

The story is found in the book of John, chapter 8. It was early morning and Jesus was teaching in the temple when the scribes and Pharisees brought the woman saying she was caught in the act of adultery. According to the Laws of Moses she should be stoned to death. The accusers cleverly asked, *"what do you think Jesus?"* Although according to their laws, she was guilty, yet their true motive was disguised underneath. Their real plan was to trap Jesus into speaking against the Law of Moses. I call this "the bait and switch," because they did not seem to care about the sin of adultery that was committed by the woman but gathering evidence to nail Christ to the cross. The man who was caught in the same act of adultery was never questioned.

"If a man commits adultery with another man's wife, with the wife of his neighbor, both the adulterer and the adulteress are to be put to death." Leviticus 20:10

Jesus basically ignored their question, looking away and writing on the ground as if he did not hear them. I wonder what was he writing, was he writing a list of the accuser's sins? Maybe he was writing their names so that the crowd could easily identify the accusers. Who knows, but whatever it was made an impact on the question that Jesus asked them.

After their continual asking, Jesus finally turned to them and said, "He who is without sin among you, let him cast the first stone." When they heard this, being convicted by the Holy Spirit in their conscience, all walked away one by one starting with the oldest to the youngest. I see this as a generational order. Those of us who are mature and have experienced life longer, have a responsibility to lead the younger generation the right way. If you know better, God is holding you responsible to do better!

Jesus then looked to the woman saying, "where are your accusers, has no one condemned you? She said, "No one Lord." And Jesus said to her, "Neither do I condemn you; go and sin no more." John 8:11

The Accuser!

The English Oxford Dictionary definition of an accuser, is a person who claims that someone has committed an offense or done something wrong. Based on scripture we know that Satan is called "the Accuser of the brethren", he is accused of the crime of deceiving the world. He is a liar, and the father of all lies. He only speaks when he wants to deceive God's people. Those of us who are believers should not willingly take on the works of Satan. The followers of Christ must be mindful of the tricks of the enemy and must resist the desire to lie or speak bad words about others. This would never be the work or the call of God, rather it is the work of Satan.

There are many stories in Bible with people being falsely accused, including Jesus, Joshua, Stephen and Moses. In the book of Acts at the end of Chapter seven Stephen was stoned to death because of his beliefs. Accusers use their voices for evil and not for good. The actions of defiling a person's name still occur today all around the world.

"God blesses those who are persecuted for doing right, for the Kingdom of Heaven is theirs. "God blesses you when people mock you and persecute you and lie about you and say all sorts of evil things against you because you are my followers." Matthew 5:10-11

In the book of John, chapter eight the scribes and Pharisees brought before Jesus a woman "who they say" was caught in the act of adultery. The accusers rallied together with their own thoughts and opinions as evidence (stones), then took pleasure in publicly humiliating this woman. According to the Bible she was caught in the act of adultery and it was lawful that she be stoned. If it had not been for God's grace, she would have been killed then and there. But God!

Jesus challenged the crowd to look at their own sins, before pointing out the sins of someone else. God challenges us to not be so quick to "pile up stones" against one another. The accusers, being both judge and jury, wanted to stone this woman without a thought of looking at their own sins. We all have sinned and fallen short of God's glory, but we tend to forget because most of the sins were or have not been exposed to the human eye. This reminds me of a song by one of my favorite gospel groups, the Williams Brothers. In the song it says, "Sweep around your own front door, before you sweep around mine." The first course of action should be to look within yourself.

"Why do you look at the speck in your brother's eye, but did not consider the plank in your own eye?" Matthew 7:3

If we first evaluate self-motives, maybe it will offer the opportunity to help heal each other instead of condemning each other. What would Jesus do?

Growing up I heard my mother quote this saying thousands of times; "if you are living in a glass house, you better not throw stones."

"Stop pointing fingers and placing blame on others. Your life can only change to the degree that you accept responsibility for it." - Dr. Steve Maraboli

Blessings to You!!!

Study Scriptures:

Accusers of adultery

*1 But Jesus went to the Mount of Olives. 2 Now early in the morning He came again into the temple, and all the people came to Him; and He sat down and taught them. 3 Then the scribes and Pharisees brought to Him a woman caught in adultery. And when they had set her in the midst, 4 they said to Him, "Teacher, this woman was caught[b] in adultery, in the very act. 5 Now Moses, in the law, commanded[c] us that such should be stoned. [d] But what do You say?" 6 This they said, testing Him, that they might have something of which to accuse Him. But Jesus stooped down and wrote on the ground with His finger, as though He did not hear. [f]
7 So when they continued asking Him, He raised Himself up[g] and said to them, "He who is without sin among you, let him throw a stone at her first." 8 And again He stooped down and wrote on the ground. 9 Then those who heard it, being*

convicted by their conscience, [h] went out one by one, beginning with the oldest even to the last. And Jesus was left alone, and the woman standing in the midst. 10 When Jesus had raised Himself up and saw no one but the woman, He said to her, "Woman, where are those accusers of yours? Has no one condemned you?" 11 She said, "No one, Lord." And Jesus said to her, "Neither do I condemn you; go and sin no more." 12 Then Jesus spoke to them again, saying, "I am the light of the world. He who follows Me shall not walk in darkness, but have the light of life."   John 8:1-12 (NKJV)

Faith Triumphs in Trouble
Therefore, having been justified by faith, we have[a] peace with God through our Lord Jesus Christ, through whom also we have access by faith into this grace in which we stand, and rejoice in hope of the glory of God. And not only that, but we also glory in tribulations, knowing that tribulation produces perseverance; and perseverance,

character; and character, hope. Now hope does not disappoint, because the love of God has been poured out in our hearts by the Holy Spirit who was given to us.

Christ in Our Place

For when we were still without strength, in due time Christ died for the ungodly. For scarcely for a righteous man will one die; yet perhaps for a good man someone would even dare to die. But God demonstrates His own love toward us, in that while we were still sinners, Christ died for us. Much more then, having now been justified by His blood, we shall be saved from wrath through Him. For if when we were enemies we were reconciled to God through the death of His Son, much more, having been reconciled, we shall be saved by His life. And not only that, but we also rejoice in God through our Lord Jesus Christ, through whom we have now received the reconciliation. - Romans 5:1-11 (NKJV)

Then I heard a loud voice shouting across the heavens, "It has come at last-- salvation and power and the Kingdom of our God, and the authority of his Christ. For the accuser of our brothers and sisters has been thrown down to earth-- the one who accuses them before our God day and night. Rev. 12:10 NLT

Chapter 2

CAUGHT IN THE ACT

> *"And you shall know the truth, and the truth shall make you free."* - John 8:32

"Teacher," they said to Jesus, "this woman was **caught in the act** *of adultery. The law of Moses says to stone her. What do you say?"* John 8:4-5

This poor woman was being publicly humiliated by the religious leaders, because she was caught committing adultery. Can you imagine the hurt shame and personal pain of having her "private sin," put on full display before the entire community? I am quite sure she did not expect the sinful act she committed behind closed doors to ever be brought out into the open light.

There are millions of others who have been "caught in the act." I recall an incident growing up about a boy in my neighborhood who stole a honeybun from the local store. When he returned home, his mother found out that he had stolen that honeybun. She was so furious that she beat and punched him all the way back to store and made him return it. Now that was public humiliation! I am sure the young boy was embarrassed and hurt that his mom was disappointed in his bad choice. Don't get me wrong, stealing is a sin and should never be taken lightly. But is it possible his mom could have handled the situation in a different way? Did she forget to remember the feeling of making a mistake? Was anger the best response? I don't want to go too far or get off the beaten path, but scripture tells us that we "all have sinned" and fallen short of God's glory. All means all!

We cannot afford to become so "willy-nilly" with sin, operating as if it has no cost or negative impact on our lives. To continually live in sin causes enslavement to the sinful lifestyle. If we take a moment and meditate in the spirit (not judging but discerning), we would probably see a lot of the pitfalls of Satan schemes. We often unnecessarily struggle as a result of the sinful, and ungodly actions prompted by the deceiver. No man is strong enough on his own to pull away from the grip and stronghold of the sins of the world. Sin does not discriminate because of wealth, class, gender or origin. It is only through the admission and repentance of our sins and through the grace of God and the blood of Jesus that we are given the "the power" to pull away from sin.

You may be able to hide the sin out of the eye sight of man (husband, wife, friends and family), but there is nothing hidden from the omnipresent God! From the very beginning man has tried to hide his sins from God. Adam tried to hide in the garden after his sin of disobedience (eating from the forbidden tree). Sarah, Abrams wife was "caught in the act" of sin with her negative contrary thoughts, when she laughed at the thought that she could birth a child in her old age. Moses was "caught in the act", committing murder, beating an Egyptian to death and hiding his dead body in the sands. Then there is David, King David, who is known as the "man after God's own heart." David could not hide from his sin of adultery with Bathsheba (another man's wife), who bore him a son. We all have committed sin in some form.

Satan roams around like a roaring lion looking for whom he may devour. Those who are weak in faith is the most vulnerable (subject to physical, emotional attack or harm). Satan is searching for the weak ones! Get up and strengthen yourself in faith through prayer and meditation of the Word of God.
We must be careful not to be so quick in judging others who are "caught in the act of sin." For surely as you live your sins will find you. When you knowing or unknowingly sin, quickly repent and ask God for His forgiveness. It is so easy to get caught up in the bad habits and thrills of life without thinking things through. The world glamorizes sin, and

so many of God's people are ready to jump right in. Try to pause for a moment and think about the consequences of your actions. A sinful life comes with repercussions.

Too many of God's people are experiencing poverty and frustration instead of prosperity and the goodness of God's manifestation. God is not in the business of chaos and he will not bless the mess that we choose to create. We often reject His will for our own will. It is time out for allowing our life to go in the opposite direct of God's perfect plan. We must stop going backwards!

God constantly delivers us from sinful people and circumstances, yet we keep stumbling right back! Slipping back into the darkness of sin causes dark thoughts to become even darker. Satan in his deceitfulness causes us to disregard the truth of God's Word. We slip back into the hole of sin and make it nearly impossible to see the light of God's glory. As Proverb 26:11 states,

"Like a dog returning to his vomit, so a fool returns to his folly."

When we know better, we should do better. Total commitment is what Christ requires of us. Although we have the option (free will) to choose righteousness, it is amazing how frequently we choose wrong. Christ has broken the chains of bondage and set us free! It is on us to take a stand and work hard to never let sin rule.

"No procrastination and no backward looks. You can't put God's kingdom off till tomorrow, but seize the day." Luke 9:62 (MSG). It is time to be steadfast, striving toward the powerful, and purposeful things of Christ that will last.

Allow me to speak prophetically; "God holds back the rain in many areas of our lives." This rain represents the outpouring of God's fresh anointing and blessings. Because of our disobedience and unwillingness to repent of our sins, He holds back the rain! I can hear it in my spirit that the drought is ending. Repentance and rejoicing can happen in this season.

There was only one who walked this earth without sin and that is Jesus Christ, the son of almighty God. So, I say to you, if you are going to get "caught in the act," be sure it is in the act of doing good. There is still time to get things right, as long as there is breath in your body and the blood is still running warm in your veins.

"Brothers and sisters, if someone is caught in a sin, you who live by the Spirit should restore that person gently. But watch yourselves, or you also may be tempted." Galatians 6:1

Wet Wood!
Definition of wet wood: wood having a water-soaked or translucent appearance because of abnormally elevated water content sometimes due to bacteria and sometimes to physiological factors.

From my studies I come to understand the unique relationship between wood and moisture. A fundamental fact is that wood has a tendency to absorb moisture from the air (hygroscopic). This means that wood, almost like a sponge, will gain or lose moisture from the air based upon the conditions of the surrounding environment. This causes wood to expand or contract based on the its surroundings or atmosphere. This is a good example of our relationship with God. If life is good and is creating an environment of joy and happiness, our relationship with God expands. In the same way if life is tough, creating an environment of pain and struggles, our relationship with God contracts. We drawback from God!

My point is for you to see the "feelings" of expanding or contracting relationships with God based on our spiritual environment. Are we cold in spirit or on fire in spirit? One thing is for certain, if there is a change or a swing in our relationship from hot to cold or dry to wet, it is because we change. God never changes!

"I am the LORD, and I do not change."
Malachi 3:6a

"God is not human, that he should lie, not a human being, that he should change his mind." Numbers 23:19a

Too many Christians have allowed the enemy to get the upper hand in their lives. This happens by straying away from the things of God. His warnings are being ignored. Now we "feel" separated from God.

When our desires for the things of the world are greater than our desires for the things of the kingdom, this is an indication that our relationship with God has grown cold and wet.

But in spite of our "wet wooded selves", the goodness of God still shines through. The most heartfelt witnessing and ministering happens when we are knee deep in the waters of life. This is where we have witnessed the fire of the Holy Spirits being stirred up in the hearts of men. In spite of the wet spiritual environment, it is never an impossibility that the Holy Spirit cannot set hearts aflame for the Lord.

1 Kings chapter 18, God sent fire from Heaven and consumed the burnt offering, the wet wood and even the stones. When the people saw this, they fell on their faces and gave witness that the Lord is God.

We all know that in the natural you cannot start a fire with wet wood, but for those of us who are true believers, know nothing is impossible for God. He can set hearts on fire and burn up the wet stuff that is prohibiting you from serving Him. All it takes is a little kindling to start a big fire!

"I know all the things you do, that you are neither hot nor cold. I wish that you

*were one or the other! But since you are
like lukewarm water, neither hot nor
cold, I will spit you out of my mouth!
Revelation 3:15-16 NLT*

We all need the Holy Spirit to the set the
fire deep down in our souls! God knows
all about you. He knew you before you
were formed in your mother's womb.
With this in mind, He knows when you
have become distant from him.   He
knows when you do not feel like
praying, praising or acknowledging him.
He knows when his process is unclear
to you. When this happens, we tend to
seek our own way and operate in our
own plans. We have turned away from
the plan, the purpose and the gifting of
God in our lives. God tenderly calls us
back by restoring and rekindling us
through prayer and meditation with the
fire and passion for kingdom work. God
has purposed work for you to do!

*"For this reason, I remind you to fan into
flame the gift of God, which is in you
through the laying on of my hands. For*

*the Spirit God gave us does not make us
timid, but gives us power, love and self-
discipline."*

- 2 Timothy 1:6-7 NIV

Holy Spirit, please ignite a fire deep
down in our souls!

Blessings to You!!!

Study Scriptures

"Keep me safe from the traps set by evildoers, from the snares they have laid for me." Psalms 141:9

"An evil man is ensnared by the transgression of his lips, But the righteous will escape from trouble." Proverbs 12:13

"But those who want to get rich fall into temptation and a snare and many foolish and harmful desires which plunge men into ruin and destruction." 1 Timothy 1:6

"Repent, then, and turn to God, so that your sins may be wiped out, that times of refreshing may come from the Lord." Acts 3:19 (NIV)

"Moses and Aaron then went into the tent of meeting. When they came out, they blessed the people; and the glory of the Lord appeared to all the people. Fire came out from the presence of the Lord and consumed the burnt offering and the

31

fat portions on the altar. And when all the people saw it, they shouted for joy and fell facedown." Lev. 3:23-24NIV

Chapter Three

PILING UP STONES

Piling up the stones is what I define as the process of the gathering of hard rocks, sinful activities or sinful things that other people do or have done. The piling up of stones could even be the conjuring up of falsehoods and lies about someone. The gathering of all this negative stuff whether it be truth or lies is all intended to persecute another person so the accuser can look or feel better and above others. "Throwing the stones," beating them down, slandering their name, destroying their reputation and potentially causing death from the heavy and hard rocks of negative trashy stuff, in an effort humiliate a person or situation. This pile of stones could even be sinful things that you know to be true but used to cause harm on another person's reputation.

"If you dig one ditch you better dig two cause the trap you set for me just may be for you."
-Mahalia Jackson

I wanted to make my definition of "piling up the stones" crystal clear, just in case you are engaged in this kind of negative trash dumping or that you have the notion to do it. Please understand that it is wrong and sinful in the eyes of God. If you are a true believer in Jesus Christ then out of your mouth should flow rivers of living waters, and not waters filled with toxic and poison stuff that damages others.

The stones (negativity) you gather up on others, could easily fall on you! The best thing for you is to gather or pile up stones to be used to strengthen the foundation of a faith walk for self and others. Also, to build walls of good stones (Word of God) to keep the enemy on the outside of your life.

Allow me to share a couple of stories, one from the Bible and a second related story from current news with illustrations of piling up the stones.

Story one

In Acts 6 and 7, Stephen was falsely accused of blasphemy, then stoned to death for simply doing good. Stephen and seven others were selected to serve the tables in order to give more time to the disciples who minister to the people. The requirement for being selected was that you had to be a man of good reputation and "full" of the Holy Spirit and wisdom. In fact, of the seven men chosen, Stephen was the only one this scripture mentioned twice. It explains that he was a man full of the Holy Spirit and though faith was executing great wonders and signs among the people. But as good as he was, opposition arose.

Have you ever noticed that when you are doing good things and even great things for the kingdom, the enemy stirs up strong opposition? The Synagogue of Freedmen (Cyrenian's and Alexandrian's) started disputing against Stephen. They induced others to lie and say they heard him speaking blasphemous words against God. It is also noted that Stephen was so full of the Spirit that when this accusing council looked at him, they saw his face as the face of an angel. In spite of all the good the people and the council saw in Stephen, all of his spiritual gifts and the anointing on his life, they resisted the truth (the spirit tugging at their hearts). They stoned him anyway. The most amazing part of the story to me is at the end (v. 59 & 60). As they were stoning Stephen, he called out not in pain, not in anger, nor in fear, but in love and forgiveness. *"Lord Jesus, receive and welcome my spirit, Lord, do not hold this sin against them.*

We Forgive the Killer
Story two
Family of Facebook live murder victim: We forgive the killer!
-Catholic News Agency - April 2017

CLEVELAND -- Mourning family members of a Cleveland man whose

*murder on Easter Sunday was posted
online in a Facebook video said that
despite their grief, they forgive their
father's killer.*

*"Each one of us forgives the killer. The
murderer. We want to wrap our arms
around him," said Tonya Godwin Baines
in a CNN interview. She said that it was
her slain father who taught her, through
the example of his life, how to forgive.*

*"The thing that I would take away the
most from my father is he taught us
about God. How to fear God. How to love
God. And how to forgive." On Sunday
afternoon, 74-year-old Robert Godwin Sr.
was shot and killed in Cleveland while
walking home from Easter dinner with
his family. Police said that the suspect,
37-year-old Steve Stephens, apparently
chose his victim at random, and then
uploaded a video of the murder to
Facebook. The social media network
later removed the video.*

This family did not pile up the stones.
Instead they leaned on God, their
Heavenly Father and showed the world

how Christians should respond in time
of tragedy and hurt. This story is a true
reflection of "God's unlimited measures
of love." The same love and forgiveness
witnessed and spoken of in the Bible
days. We all should learn to love our
fellow man, our neighbors as ourselves.

This next story shows the love and
forgiveness of Jesus. In fact, it
encouraged me to write this book. The
narrative tells of a woman guilty of
committing adultery; caught in the very
act but she was not stoned.

Back in ancient Israel stoning was a
method of capital punishment for
people who broke specific statues of the
law of Moses. Acts punishable by
stoning were disobedience, blasphemy,
working on the Sabbath, worship of
false gods and adultery. We all should
thank God for the new and better
covenant that allows for repentance
and forgives our sins. This generation
of man would all be stoned to death
based on the list in Moses law.

In the gospel of John chapter 8, it is early morning and Jesus is teaching in the Temple. The scribes and Pharisees brought a woman and claimed she was caught in the act of adultery should be stoned. The accusers cleverly asked, "what do you think Jesus?" Their plan was to trap Jesus into speaking against the Laws of Moses.

They really did not care as much about the sin of adultery committed by the woman as much as they were in trying to disparage the reputation of Jesus. Of course, the woman was never accused of any wrongdoing. Jesus ignored their question, looking away and writing on the ground as if he did not hear them. After their continual asking, Jesus finally turned to them and said, *"He who is with sin among you, let him cast the first stone."*
When they heard this, being convicted by the Holly Spirit, all walked away. *Jesus then looked to women saying, "where are your accusers, has no one*

condemned you? She said, "No one
Lord." And Jesus said to her, "Neither do I
condemn you; go and sin no more."
First look within yourself and take note
of your own sinfulness. We are quick to
look at the speck in our brother's eye,
but rarely consider the plank in our
own eye?

*"A self-absorbed person only can see the
faults of others, but often time color blind to
their own."*   - -
InstaQuote

Blessing to You!!!

Study Scriptures:

Israel Resists the Holy Spirit

51 "You stiff-necked and uncircumcised in heart and ears! You always resist the Holy Spirit; as your fathers did, so do you. 52 Which of the prophets did your fathers not persecute? And they killed those who foretold the coming of the Just One, of whom you now have become the betrayers and murderers, 53 who have received the law by the direction of angels and have not kept it."
Stephen the Martyr
54 When they heard these things they were cut to the heart, and they gnashed at him with their teeth. 55 But he, being full of the Holy Spirit, gazed into heaven and saw the glory of God, and Jesus standing at the right hand of God, 56 and said, "Look! I see the heavens opened and the Son of Man standing at the right hand of God!"
57 Then they cried out with a loud voice, stopped their ears, and ran at him with one accord; 58 and they cast him out of

the city and stoned him. And the witnesses laid down their clothes at the feet of a young man named Saul. 59 And they stoned Stephen as he was calling on God and saying, "Lord Jesus, receive my spirit." 60 Then he knelt down and cried out with a loud voice, "Lord, do not charge them with this sin." And when he had said this, he fell asleep." ACTS 7:51-60 (NKJV)

"These are the things you shall do: Speak each man the truth to his neighbor; Give judgment in your gates for truth, justice, and peace; Let none of you think evil in your[a] heart against your neighbor; And do not love a false oath. For all these are things that I hate,' Says the Lord." Zachariah 8:16-17 (NKJV) "The guilty walk a crooked path; the innocent travel a straight road." Psalms 21:8 (NLT)

"Do not fret because of those who are evil or be envious of those who do wrong; for

like the grass they will soon wither, like green plants they will soon die away. Trust in the Lord and do good; dwell in the land and enjoy safe pasture. Take delight in the Lord,
and he will give you the desires of your heart." Psalms 37:1-4 NLT

Chapter Four

WHAT DO YOU SAY?

"Teacher," they said to Jesus, "this woman was caught in the act of adultery. 5 The law of Moses says to stone her. What do you say?"6 They were trying to trap him into saying something they could use against him, but Jesus stooped down and wrote in the dust with his finger. John 8:4-6 (NLT)

Before Jesus answered the question from the Pharisees, he stooped down and wrote on the ground. I wonder what did Jesus write in the dirt? Is it scripture? Did He note the Pharisees by name? Was it simply scribbling in the dirt? Is it possible he was just taking time to reflect before responding? Maybe he was giving them time to consider their own sinful acts and not be so quick to judge. This is what we all should do before reacting to any situation. Prayer and meditation.

What do you say? The scribes and Pharisees were expecting Jesus to say something, anything that would be contrary to the Law of Moses so they could trap and accuse him of being an enemy to the law. They were testing Jesus to see if he would contradict his own nature for good. If you notice, the scribes and Pharisees did not ask Jesus what he would do, but what does he have to say. They were hopeful that his words would incriminate him.

Isn't this just the way the world thinks today? We constantly put each other on the spot for doing something or saying something good or bad. The world excites in accusing anyone who may be caught up in sinful living. We all have to admit sometimes good people do bad (sinful) things! If you were punished for every wrong and sinful act you committed, there wouldn't be much skin left from all the stone blows.

Be careful what you say about others. Words carry a great deal of weight. Words can be the lightness of blessings or the heaviness of cursing. There really is power in your words! Words can draw a crowd or insight a riot. We

> "And I tell you this, you must give an account on judgment day for every idle word you speak. The words you say will either acquit you or condemn you."
> Matthew 12:36-37 (NLT)

should be ever so watchful of every word that comes out of our mouth, it will do just what you purposed it to do.

Are the words spoken from your mouth representative of your godly character? What do your words say about you? Do they shine light in the time of darkness or do your words create the darkness?

With his words, Martin Luther King empowered a nation and fueled the world for right thinking, love and unity. His words inspired the nation to lean toward the righteousness of God, when he said I have a dream. *"I have a dream that one day little black boys and girls will be holding hands with little white boys and girls."*

President John F. Kennedy mobilized the nation when he set a dramatic goal and cast his vision of a man walking on the moon. *"This nation should commit itself to achieving the goal, before the decade is out, of landing a man on the moon and returning him safely to the earth."*

With His word, Jesus Christ set an adulterous woman free. In doing so He set the world free from the feeling of guilt, shame and the punishment of death. We have direct access to God through Christ Jesus to repent and seek forgiveness. His words set us free when He said, *"not my will Lord, but thy will be done."*

Your words are precious seeds that infiltrate the atmosphere for good or for evil. These powerful words can cause a change in the atmosphere and affect those around you. When your words are mixed with faith you can speak to the mountains (obstacles) of life, and they will have to move out of the way. Today is the day to speak to your mountains of debt, doubt, fear, bondage, un-forgiveness or judgement and command them to move.

God expects us to speak His words so that it will be passed on for many generations. We should speak more about God and use the word of God to cover or handle any and all situations. Not our words, but His word.

Change your words and you can change your world!

Wounded by Words!

You better watch your words! This is what my mother would say to us when we spoke profanity about something or someone. She would then follow up by saying, "I am going to wash your mouth out with soap." At the time we thought that was just another threat from mom to make a house of five boys behave better. We would laugh to ourselves and say, how is she going to wash our mouths with soap? It was funny back then, but now we understand the ramifications of idle words. Mother understood the cause and effect, the negative impact and destructive power of these negative words. She wanted to clean it up from the root!

We all have heard the old saying that "sticks and stones may break my bones, but words will never hurt me." Well, you know this is not the truth; words do hurt, they have power to bless or curse, to heal or harm.

In today's society some people choose to use social media as a means for verbal attacks. There seems to not be a limit to the disgraceful and hurt words spoken at or about another human being while online. In some cases, there is total disrespect for self and others. This forum can also be used as a way to bully others creating a massive and quicker impact. Bullying is linked to many negative outcomes especially on a child's well-being, including mental health, substance abuse, and suicide.

Millions of people have been wounded by words that were spoken to them or about them. But thank God for a way of escape. We have the God given power to reverse the curse of bad words spoken over us. Speaking the Word of God washes and cleanses the soul.

"Life and death are in the power of the tongue." Prov. 18:21

The words that are conceived in the heart, then formed by the tongue, and spoken out of the mouth, becomes a spiritual force releasing the ability of God within you. Words are one of the most powerful things in the universe. The words spoken can pull you over or hold you under. We must learn to use our words wisely.

We have used our own tongue to form the very words that defeat us. We have prayed prayers of defeat and received it! We spoke our problems and became it. Word are seed that produces after its own kind.

Speak as the Word tells us;

I am the head and not the tail, above and not beneath.

I am more than a conqueror.

I am the righteousness of God.
I can do all things through Christ which strengthens me.

This is the right way to use the power of your words to bless yourself and others.

James 3:10 says *out of the same mouth come blessings or curses.*

The words you speak are working for you or against you based on what you say! Don't speak words that are contrary to the will of God, change the atmosphere with words of blessings, love and peace, not curses. "Be careful what you say about other, knowingly or unknowingly you are setting the same atmosphere for yourself."

"Your time is limited, so don't waste it living someone else's life. Don't be trapped by dogma — which is living with the results of what other people think. Don't let the noise of others' opinions drown out your own inner voice. And most important, have the courage to

follow your heart and intuition. They somehow already know what you truly want to become. Everything else is secondary".
-Steve Jobs.

Blessings to You!!!

Study Scriptures:

"Truly I tell you, if anyone says to this mountain, 'Go, throw yourself into the sea,' and does not doubt in their heart but believes that what they say will happen, it will be done for them." Mark 11:23 (NIV)

"Death and life are in the power of the tongue: and they that love it shall eat the fruit thereof."
Proverbs 8:21 (KJV)

"Continue earnestly in prayer, being vigilant in it with thanksgiving; meanwhile praying also for us, that God would open to us a door for the word, to speak the mystery of Christ, for which I am also in chains, that I may make it manifest, as I ought to speak.
Walk in wisdom toward those who are outside, redeeming the time. Let your speech always be with grace, seasoned with salt, that you may know how you ought to answer each one."
Colossians 4:2-6 (NKJV)

"The mouth of the righteous flows with wisdom, But the perverted tongue will be cut out."
Proverbs 10:31
"When she speaks, her words are wise, and she gives instructions with kindness."
Proverbs 31:26

21 "As for Me," says the Lord, "this is My covenant with them: My Spirit who is upon you, and My words which I have put in your mouth, shall not depart from your mouth, nor from the mouth of your descendants, nor from the mouth of your descendants' descendants," says the Lord, "from this time and forevermore." Isaiah 59:21 NLT

Chapter Five

FALSELY ACCUSED

Wikipedia defines "false accusation" as insufficient supporting evidence to determine whether an accusation is true or false, it is described as "unsubstantiated" or "unfounded"

False allegations levied on anyone is hard!

Let us take a close look into the story of Job. The scripture tells us he was blameless and upright; he feared God and shunned evil. He was a wealthy man, with seven sons and three daughters, owning several thousand head of livestock and having a large number of servants. Job was a godly man and the godly priest of his household. Routinely after family gatherings and periods of feasting he would purify his family through prayer and burnt offerings. This was done not so much based on the sins of the family, but out of Job's love, devotion and commitment to God. He was known as the greatest man among all the people in the east because of his wealth, his love for God and love for family.

There was a second affirmation of Job's greatness of character, when the Lord said to Satan, *"Have you tested my servant Job? There is no one on earth like him; he is blameless and upright, a man who fears God and shuns evil."* To this Satan replied, *"you built a hedge all around him and his household. You blessed the work of his hand to cause wealth and to multiply and spread across the land. If you lift your hand of protection from covering Job, he will curse you to your face."*

It is astounding to see how clearly Satan can see our blessings and how far he is willing to go to disrupt the flow of our blessings. But that is a message for another day! Job endured tests, troubles and trials and lost everything he cherished in life. He lost his family of seven children and his wife. To top it off he lost all of his worldly possessions and riches. A point worth noting is he did not lose his soul! Job's testing, heartaches and heartbreaks was bad enough, then came the false accusations from his three closest friends. After a brief period of lamenting and comforting with Job, they each in their own way accused Job of sinning against God. Elipahz saw Job's suffering as punishment resulting from his sins. He even claimed to have some divine revelation from God on this matter.

> "Surely, he recognizes deceitful men; and when he sees Evelin, does he not take note?
> Job 11:11

Bildad made the assumptions that Job's children died because of their sins and wickedness. His presumption was that Job trusted more in own his riches than he did in God. Zophar came at Job full throttle, not just piling on the stones, but throwing the stones of false accusations at Job, by saying that Job deserved even more punishment. He accused Job of hiding secret faults and sins.

You may have had an experience of family or friends turning their back on you and can relate to the feeling. This is exactly the next move Satan used to manipulate Job's wife into turning against him. In the midst of Job's suffering, his wife questioned his spiritual purity; *"are you still holding onto your integrity? Curse God and die.* But Job replied, *"You talk like a foolish woman. Should we accept only good things from the hand of God and never anything bad?"* *(Job 2:10 NLT)*
There are no limits as to how far Satan will go to reach you. Nothing is off limits! The story ends with God

rebuking the three friends for adding to Job's suffering with false accusations and judgmental attitudes. Elipahz, Bildad and Zophar presented a burnt offering to Job for their sins and asked Job to pray for them. After Job showed the act of forgiveness by praying for his friends, the Lord anointed him with prosperity by giving him twice as much as he had before. I like to say Job "received double for all of his troubles." In this story Job's periods of doubt and confusion are recognizable. Through it all he stayed in communion with God. We must do this also when we experience low periods in life. Stay on your knees until God lifts you up.

In the face of false accusations and people "piling up the stones" against you, it is important to handle things as God has instructed. We should never repay evil for evil but be steadfast and always abounding in the work of the Lord. God's love and promises are bigger than any disappointment we may face. God is bigger than the pains and the shame of life. Always know like Job, you will be rewarded in due season.

There are a number of life lessons to be learned from this part of the Job's story. First, good people have to deal with trials and tribulations of this dark world even when they are upright and of good rapport. Second, there is a tendency to lean on human understanding when it comes to understanding the ordeals of others. We tend to perceive the trials of others from our own viewpoint which is generally driven by the ways of the world. The ways of the world contrast with how God handles the setbacks of His Saints. Just as Job, we all may have to deal with being falsely accused at some point in life. I wrote about the life experience of Stephen who was falsely accused of blasphemy and eventually stoned to death in the first chapter of this book. But with his dying breath Stephen asked God for forgiveness for his accusers. In the midst this horrific punishment, God was still glorified.

To be falsely accused is hurtful and frustrating! The accusations are generally presumptions or assumptions driven by ignorance, jealousy and hatred.

"Blessed are ye, when men shall revile you, and persecute you, and shall say all manner of evil against you falsely, for my sake". Matthew 5:11 (KJV)

It is much too easy to allow the heart to become as hard as stone. Hard Hearted! The enemy deceives the view of right and wrong. Seeing self as right and someone else as wrong is what can be defined as self-righteousness. When this happens, we enter into the "danger zone." This is a mental zone for a high risk of harming self and others. It is dangerous in the sense that we are willing to ignore the feelings and lives of others which can cause hurt, shame or pain.

It is our stubbornness that can hinder change, thus causing us not to grow and be the best we can be. In seeing only our personal perspectives matters in life is not our best. It is wise to look deep into ourselves in an effort not to take unforgiveness and hard heartedness to the grave. I would hope not to leave this type of intolerant behavior to the next generation. If the shoe fits, remember you don't have to wear it! Try to forgive as much as you can and as often as you can. Your life and the life of others will be better for it.

"I shall pass through this world but once. Any good Therefore that I can do or any kindness that I can show to any human being, let me do it now. Let me not defer or neglect, for I shall not pass this way again." - Mahatma Gandhi

Don't Let Life Troubles Define You!

We are all faced with trials, troubles and tribulations of this life. No one is exempt from the struggles of this world;

be it broken heart, broken relationships or just down right broken financially. These conflicts of life are inevitable, for without the conflict and complications of life, we would not sense the need for God. Without the warfare and battles of life, there would be no reason for us to be called by God as conquerors. In fact, His Word says that we are more than conquerors in Christ Jesus.

It is through struggles, that we gain strength! Struggles draw us closer to God, although none of us want to go through challenges, God has a way of working all things out for good.

Sometimes struggles are needed to get our will in line and detach our minds from the day to day grind of life. God uses this time to prune and refine the matters of our mind.

James 1:2-4 (NIV) *"Consider it pure joy, my brothers and sisters, whenever you face trials of many kinds, because you know that the testing of your faith produces perseverance. Let perseverance finish its work so that you may be mature and complete, not lacking anything."*

God already knows about our struggles and has equipped us to handle them. Don't waste any more time focusing on your problem, put your mind and your focus on the power of your God. It is in our weakness that His strength is made perfect!

There is a familiar scripture that I personally lean on when I am dealing with my life struggles and that is Romans 8:28, *"And we know that in all things God works for the good of those who love him, who have been called according to his purpose."*

God is aware of the bad things or the bad circumstances in our lives, but you can trust that He will make all things work out for your good.

Through struggles we gain our strength. When faced with the rigorous winds of life, remember it is to strengthen your wings in preparation for you to take flight. It is the way to break free of constraints and restraints of life. Our struggles should not define us, but God will use them to refine us!

Blessings to You!!!

Henry Ford Quotes, "When everything seems to be going against you, remember that the airplane takes off against the wind, not with it."

Study Scriptures:

Behave Like a Christian
"Let love be without hypocrisy. Abhor what is evil. Cling to what is good. Be kindly affectionate to one another with brotherly love, in honor giving preference to one another; not lagging in diligence, fervent in spirit, serving the Lord; rejoicing in hope, patient in tribulation, continuing steadfastly in prayer; distributing to the needs of the saints, given to hospitality.

Bless those who persecute you; bless and do not curse. Rejoice with those who rejoice, and weep with those who weep. Be of the same mind toward one another. Do not set your mind on high things, but associate with the humble. Do not be wise in your own opinion.

Repay no one evil for evil. Have regard for good things in the sight of all men. If it is possible, as much as depends on you, live peaceably with all men. Beloved, do not avenge yourselves, but rather give place to wrath; for it is written, "Vengeance is Mine, I will repay,"[a] says

the Lord. Therefore, "If your enemy is hungry, feed him; If he is thirsty, give him a drink;
For in so doing you will heap coals of fire on his head."[b] Do not be overcome by evil, but overcome evil with good. - Romans 12:8-21 (NKJV)

"You must not pass along false rumors. You must not cooperate with evil people by lying on the witness stand. "You must not follow the crowd in doing wrong. When you are called to testify in a dispute, do not be swayed by the crowd to twist justice. And do not slant your testimony in favor of a person just because that person is poor. Exodus 23:1-3 (NLT)

Chapter Six

NEITHER DO I

As stated in the introduction of this book, I believe the greatest gift ever given is the gift of forgiveness. God gave His only son to die on the cross, even while we were yet sinners. Think on this statement for a moment, guilty, but forgiven. We are guilty of wallowing in sin, yet Jesus was bruised for our iniquities, shared His blood, and gave His life so the entire world could be saved from its own sinfulness.

> "But He was wounded for our transgressions, He was bruised for our iniquities;
> The chastisement for our peace was upon Him, And by His stripes we are healed."
> Isaiah 53:5 (NKJV)

In the Gospel of John chapter eight, there is a woman on who scripture gave no name to but labeled as the "adulterous woman." Thinking forward this could be a number of women or men in today's society. What I find interesting is that, this woman according to the scripture was "caught" in the very act of adultery (sin). Her accusers were presumably eyewitnesses to this act of sin, they then pled their case before Jesus. They tested Jesus by commanding that she be stoned! He listened to their every word, which clearly convicted this woman of adultery. The men thought in their minds that Jesus would hold to the strictest "Laws of Moses," which meant she would be found guilty and then stoned to death. After Jesus heard enough, He turned the case on its hills by saying, *"anyone of you who is without sin, let him throw the first stone."* The men were convicted in their hearts and began to walk away, one by one, until they were all gone.

When Jesus stood, he saw no one but the woman and said to her, *"Woman, where are those accusers of yours. Has no one condemned you?"* She said, *"No one, Lord."* And Jesus said to her, *"Neither do I condemn you; go and sin no more."* John 8:10-11 (NKJV)

Jesus seized every event and every moment in His earthly journey as a teachable moment. In this instance, He taught the Scribes and Pharisees to look within themselves first, to see their own sin and to deal with their own self-righteousness before finding fault in others. It was their darkness (sins) that was seeking to perpetuate darkness on others. But Jesus shined His light on them so they might see their own wicked ways.

Also, Jesus showed the woman that all had sinned and if they were willing to confess their sins, He was willing and able to forgive them of their sins at that very moment.

"Neither do I, go and sin no more."

"If we say that we have no sin, we deceive ourselves and the truth is not in us. If we confess our sins, He is faithful and just to forgive us of our sins and cleanse us from all un-righteousness." 1John 1:8-9 (NKJV)

Like this woman we all have sinned and fallen short of the glory of God. Be it committing a sinful act, harboring bitterness, slinging evil words or hosting evil thoughts, we all have sinned. Thanks be to God this is not the end of our story, it's the beginning of our greater story. A life story of redemption! God wants to cleanse us of our sins and all unrighteousness. There is nothing too hard, and no sin too big that God cannot handle. But we too must do our part by:

- Confessing the sin
- Repenting the sin
- Turning away from sin
- Getting rid of bitterness and anger
- Forgiving others who have wronged you

The reward for doing these things is much greater than the sacrifice of taking these steps. The good thing is, we don't have to go through this alone. God sends the Holy Spirit to guide, provide, and protect us. The Holy Spirit is our helper in this journey! Now all we have to do is follow.

Not Guilty!
Satan the accuser of the brethren, reminds of us of past and present sins. He does this to keep man in emotional bondage, powerless, and operating in fear. Stop beating yourself up, you are no longer under the law, but under Grace!

Let me remind you, there is no condemnation for those who belong to Christ Jesus. We are free from the "law of sin and death," which means, although we may commit sin, the Law no longer has dominion over us. It is all because of the finished work of Jesus on the cross. As a believer we are not only free from bondage of sin, we are free from the inner emotions, thoughts, feelings and weightiness of sin. We are innocent of all accusations. There is no sentence inflicted and no guilty verdict is found.

"By the grace of God, believers in Jesus Christ will not face the condemnation of God. "We have passed from death to life" (1 John 3:14).

You may have sin in your life but thank God sin does not have you. Jesus has already paid the price, so you don't have to pay. *"Neither do I, go and sin no more."*

Life is short, Break the Rules. Forgive quickly, Kiss slowly. Love truly. Laugh uncontrollably and never regret ANYTHING That makes you smile. -Mark Twain

The Unspoken Verdict!
We are convicted in our spirit long before any verdict by a judge or jury. There is no place within us for our sins to hide! The Spirit of God within us is our conscience. It acts as a moral compass to distinguish right from wrong. The Spirit gives off a warning signal in our subconscious. It urges us

to do right, even when we consciously want to do wrong. If we choose to do wrong, the Spirit, convicts us and makes it plain that we have sinned. Those tough days you face and often times those sleepless nights are a result of the lingering feeling of un-repented sin. If you are dealing with these feelings, confess your sins and repent of them. God is standing eagerly by to cleanse you of all your unrighteousness. The quicker we acknowledge our need for God's forgiveness the quicker we can get life back on track and in line with the will and the plan of God. He will give back joy and peace if we trust Him to forgive our sins.

"For I know my transgressions, and my sin is ever before me." Psalms 51:3

The New You!
Stop trying to mold yourself into the image of others by pretending to be someone that you are not. Don't do things outside of your true character. If

you are going imitate anybody, be sure you imitate the only somebody who is worthy, Jesus Christ!

"You were taught, with regard to your former way of life, to put off your old self. The self- corrupted by its deceitful desires; to be made new in the attitude of your minds; and to put on the new self, created to be like God in true righteousness and holiness." -Ephesians 4:22-24

We will go through many changes in this life, but this change is the real deal, a supernatural makeover from the inside that shows on the outside. A brand new you! You may resemble the old you on the outside, but on the inside its all new. The old you before you believed in Christ is completely gone. Today you are fully clothed with a new life in Christ! You now have a new way, a new walk and a new talk!

Therefore, if anyone is in Christ, the new creation has come: The old has gone, the new is here! All this is from God, who reconciled us to himself through Christ and gave us the ministry of reconciliation: that God was reconciling the world to himself in Christ, not counting people's sins against them. And he has committed to us the message of reconciliation." 2 Cor. 5:17-19

Take a look inside and make that change to the real you, the authentic you, the you that is created in the image of the Almighty God. Through the power and ministry of reconciliation, God restores you to your rightful kingdom place. The greater blessing is understanding that He is not counting your sins against you.

"There is no condemnation for those who are in Christ Jesus. Romans 8:1 Let it go! God is not counting your sins against you, then why should you. We should not allow Satan to stain our minds with the sins from the past.

God wants you to experience Him in a deeper way through his Holy Spirit. We have to free our minds and be consciously aware of God's divine purpose for our lives. Learn to follow the lead of the Holy Spirit inside of you.

Blessings to You!!!

Study Scriptures:

"If you forgive those who sin against you, your heavenly Father will forgive you. 15 But if you refuse to forgive others, your Father will not forgive your sins." Matthew 6:14-15 (NLT)

"Yet it was our weaknesses he carried; it was our sorrows that weighed him down. And we thought his troubles were a punishment from God a punishment for his own sins! But he was pierced for our rebellion, crushed for our sins. He was beaten so we could be whole. He was whipped so we could be healed. All of us, like sheep, have strayed away. We have left God's paths to follow our own. Yet the Lord laid on him the sins of us all. He was oppressed and treated harshly, yet he never said a word. He was led like a lamb to the slaughter. And as a sheep is silent before the shearers, he did not open his mouth." Isaiah 53:4-7 (NLT)

"Who is a God like You, pardoning iniquity, And passing over the

transgression of the remnant of His heritage? He does not retain His anger forever, Because He delights in mercy. He will again have compassion on us, and will subdue our iniquities. You will cast all our sins, Into the depths of the sea."
Micah 7:18-19 (NKJV)

"But those things which God foretold by the mouth of all His prophets, that the Christ would suffer, He has thus fulfilled. Repent therefore and be converted, that your sins may be blotted out, so that times of refreshing may come from the presence of the Lord." Acts 3:18-19 (NKJV)

"Since God chose you to be the holy people he loves, you must clothe yourselves with tenderhearted mercy, kindness, humility, gentleness, and patience. Make allowance for each other's faults, and forgive anyone who offends you. Remember, the Lord forgave you, so you must forgive others." - Colossians 3:12-13 (NLT)

Chapter 7

SIN NO MORE

"When the accusers heard this, they slipped away one by one, beginning with the oldest, until only Jesus was left in the middle of the crowd with the woman. Then Jesus stood up again and said to the woman, "Where are your accusers? Didn't even one of them condemn you?"
"No, Lord," she said. And Jesus said, "Neither do I. Go and sin no more." John 8:9-11 (NLT)

We can become so comfortable living in sin, that we began to think this is the right way to live; Not so! Sin is still sin and the wages of sin is still death; for some it is physical death and for others it is spiritual death. Either way it is a separation from the plan and the will of God.

"Go and sin no more", in other words, move, depart, get away from this place and away from the people or the things that causes you to sin. Be it friend or foe! Do not continue in the self-centered path that leads you astray.

Place greater trust in the Word of God and he will show you the better way. When Jesus uses the word "go", he is not saying it harshly, like get out my face. This would not be in line with His godly (loving and forgiving) character. Jesus is saying, go in my grace, go in my forgiveness and go in my blessings. Walk out of the darkness of sin and into my light of peace and purpose as I have ordained for your life. Go and sin no more!

> *"Sin is no longer master. Instead, you live under the freedom of God's grace."*

God wants to put a "hard stop," on our sinful ways. Push away, run away, and break away from sin, whatever it takes to remove yourself from the tempter. Just do it! We may even stumble and fall in the process of trying to separate ourselves from sin, but Jesus's un-failing grace and mercy will be there to pick us up again.

I believe the word go, is more of a command than an option for this woman. In her case, Jesus extended his mercy and his forgiveness and demands her holiness. Living a life of holiness will cost something, but the cost is far less than what you gain from it. Letting go of all bad spirit will reveal to mankind a world of kindness and love. There is a peace unspeakable and joy unimaginable!

Jesus paid the price with His life on the cross at Calvary for the sins of the world. So why would we think that forgiveness of sin comes free to each of one of us? Your cost of admission is your wholehearted repentance, followed by your obedience to the command (Word) of God. "Obedience is better than sacrifice."

A Prophetic Word;

It is not just about you; there are so many others whose destiny is tied to your destiny and blessings connected to your blessings. The same holds true that your sin is tied to someone else's sin. But all glory belongs to God because the Lord works behind the scene disconnecting spiritual entanglements that sin has caused. God sets us free from the judgement and the punishment of sin. The Spirit of the Lord also works to reconnect all to his network of abundant blessings. Take heed this day, "Go and sin no more."

Trouble in My Way!

I have found that trouble shows up anytime I am doing kingdom work. For me, trouble is an indicator that the work I am doing is right in line with God's divine purpose for my life. Trouble is a warning sign that something big (good) is about to happen through me or for me. I remind myself of God's promises and rewards as I continue to do His work. I believe

He will exceedingly and abundantly give me more than I can ask or think!

I know it is good to read the scriptures that speaks of God's great rewards. This is what God's Anointed Word is purposed to do; inspire, motivate, encourage, enlighten, direct and convict you. We still have to deal with the battles within ourselves even when we know of God's promises and rewards.

We are born into a world of darkness filled with bitterness, hatred and self-centeredness. Our soul man wants to take control of our Spirit man. This thought may sound like it is deep philosophy but it is simple and clear. Man's sinful nature desires to fight for control in every stage of our daily lives. There is a constant war that rages within us. It is the battle of "Good vs. Evil."

"And I know that nothing good lives in me, that is, in my sinful nature. [a] I want to do what is right, but I can't. I want to

do what is good, but I don't. I don't want to do what is wrong, but I do it anyway. But if I do what I don't want to do, I am not really the one doing wrong; it is sin living in me that does it." - Roman 7: 18-20 (NLT)

It is sometimes difficult to do right even when we know what is the right thing is to do. The soul wants to go left, but the spirit man pulls us back to do what is right.

Winston Churchill is quoted as saying, *"When there is no enemy within, the enemies outside cannot hurt you."*

It has been said that our greatest personal challenge comes from the enemy (in-a-me) within us. The good news is when God created the spirit man, he gave us dominion over all things on the earth including authority of the soul and the body.

We go to sleep with sinful thoughts but through God's amazing grace, we can awake early the next morning with good thoughts, songs, psalms and lyrical hymns of praise within our spirit. I am reminded of the lyrics from the song, by gospel artists Luther Barnes; *"Trouble in my way, I have to cry sometime. I lay awake at night, but that's alright, I know Jesus will fix it after while."*

In John chapter 17, Jesus prays to the Father to not take us out of this world, but to protect us in this world from the evil one and our own evil thoughts. Therefore, we are in this world but not of this world.

A Clean Heart!
Sin's primary purpose is to mix up the mind and ruin a righteous life. When sin is allowed in, it brings with it a weightiness, a burden, that is always too heavy to carry. After a sinful act, the devil positions negative thoughts in our mind which often generate negative feelings of being separated from God.

If you are feeling separated from God, it is because you moved, not God. In these

desperate and depressive moments of life, the Holy Spirit will cover you and God will draw you back through the power of his love and Grace when you humbly ask for help. This is the great time to "cry out to God."
"Lord, speak to my heart, if I don't hear from you, then I don't know what to do."
-Donnie McClurkin

In Psalms 51:10-11 King David prayed, *"Create in me a clean heart, O God; and renew a right spirit within me. Cast me not away from thy presence; and take not thy holy spirit from me."*

Like David, we too must ask God to blot out our sins from within, and align our heart, mind and soul, with His Spirit and His will. He can release the negativity that sin causes. Constantly connecting to God will cleanse our inner most being, so we can feel the love of his uttermost! If you are willing, then God is willing to change the chaos hidden deep inside of you. "Confessions are good for the soul." Blessings to You!

Study Scriptures:

"But Samuel replied, "What is more pleasing to the Lord, your burnt offerings and sacrifices or your obedience to his voice? Listen! Obedience is better than sacrifice, and submission is better than offering the fat of rams." 1 Samuel 15:22 NLT

"Do not let sin control the way you live; [a] do not give in to sinful desires. Do not let any part of your body become an instrument of evil to serve sin. Instead, give yourselves completely to God, for you were dead, but now you have new life. So, use your whole body as an instrument to do what is right for the glory of God. Sin is no longer your master, for you no longer live under the requirements of the law. Instead, you live under the freedom of God's Grace. Well then, since God's grace has set us free from the law, does that mean we can go on sinning? Of course not! Don't you realize that you become the slave of whatever you choose to obey? You can be

a slave to sin, which leads to death, or you can choose to obey God, which leads to righteous living. Thank God! Once you were slaves of sin, but now you wholeheartedly obey this teaching we have given you. Now you are free from your slavery to sin, and you have become slaves to righteous living." -Romans 6:12- 18 NLT

You are now ashamed of the things you used to do, things that end in eternal doom.

"But now you are free from the power of sin and have become slaves of God. Now you do those things that lead to holiness and result in eternal life. For the wages of sin is death, but the free gift of God is eternal life through Christ Jesus our Lord." -Romans 6:22-23 NLT

Chapter Eight

HURTING PEOPLE

We all have heard it said many times of hurting people hurting other people. So, when you meet a person who hurts others, if you take the time to probe deep enough you will find that person was hurt by someone else.

When you look at the hurtful things that are happening all around our cities, our country and the world, it is a clear indication that there are a lot of hurting and misguided people on this earth. This is one of the major factors behind all the violence and hatred that pummel our news each day.

> *When you look deeply into your anger, you will see that the person you call your enemy is also suffering. As soon as you see that, the capacity for accepting and having compassion for them is there."*
> *-Thich Nhat Hanh*

Satan toys with the mind of men at all times. His ugly thoughts can make you think the person standing next to you is the enemy. Not True! We have to quickly come to grips that it is the enemy (Satan) who plays mind games. He deceitfully influences mankind to cause hate, hurt and destruction. This all comes from miss guided hate that is normally a derivative of personal hurt!

"The thief comes to steal, to kill, and to destroy. I have come that they may have life and have it more abundantly." - John 10:10

Let us be very clear, Satan is real. He is the enemy and his mission is obviously destruction. He uses his power of deception to turn the hearts of men against each other only to disrupt and destroy their lives. Satan works to turn the truth (scripture) inside out with lies and deceit. He tried to trick and tempt Jesus in chapter 4:3 of Matthew. *"If You are the son of God, command that these stones become bread."* Jesus replied, *"It is written: "Man shall not live on bread alone, but on every word that comes from the mouth of God."*

In the book of Matthew 3:16-17, John baptized Jesus. When Jesus came up from the water the heavens opened up and the Spirit of God descended like a dove upon him and a voice from heaven spoke, "*this is my beloved Son, in whom I am well pleased.*" The scripture left no doubt that Jesus knew who he was. We too have to build this confidence and assurance within ourselves to recognize when the enemy is trying to sway us away from the truth.

We must study the Word consistently to show ourselves approved in order to rightly divide (have full understanding of) the word of God. Our faith in the Word will help heal and mend broken spirits. We can no longer allow evil spirits of destruction and deception to pull us away from the fruits of the spirit. We are the chosen generation and we are set apart by God. God's plan is to prosper us and not harm us, to give us hope and a great future. He wants to heal our wounds and make us a whole Holy nation. America describes itself as, "the land of the free and the home of the brave," but the Word of God illustrates the real hope of true democracy.

I have heard it said before that the first step to healing is recognizing there is a wound. Once we acknowledge the wound then there will be a greater possibility of healing.

Darkness cannot drive out darkness; only light can do that. Hate cannot conquer hate; only love can do that. Love conquers all!
"I believe that even amid today's mortar burst and whining bullets, there is still hope for the brighter tomorrow. I believe that wounded justice, lying prostrate on the blood-flowing streets of our nations, can be lifted from this dust of shame to reign supreme among the children of men." -Martin Luther King Jr.

There is greater healing beyond the physical realm. It begins and ends with the spiritual. Healing must begin in our hearts and minds. To love your neighbor is the simplest of God's command but having love for all mankind is God's greater plan.

We go out of our way to cover up the hurt. Some people use that negative energy to take control and try to dominate other people in every situation. Some people simply go along to get along in hopes of not being noticed. They do not want others to see their hurt. Sometimes the damage from hurting is hidden so deeply that it makes it difficult to find one's true self. Yet there are those who will take the negativity from pain and turn it into something positive. They witness and give testimonies of the goodness and grace of God to help get past the pain. Positive energy can help heal others.

The adulterous woman in the Gospel of John chapter 8, was totally exposed when the scribes and Pharisees singled her out in the mist of the crowd. Her sin was broadcasted publicly around the community. She was the "gossip" of the town. In fact, 2,000 years later, we are still talking about her sins. But by the favor and goodwill of God, this woman's greatest pain became her greatest gain.

Our biggest challenge is to take off the mask of pretense! We try hard at covering the hurt but it does not work. God knows and sees our pain. He wants us to acknowledge the hurt so the healing process can begin. Hidden behind the pain is God's promise of healing. What is your cover up?

Through your greatest pain, you can experience life's greatest gains!

Anointed but Troubled!

"For our struggle is not against flesh and blood, but against the rulers, against the authorities, against the powers of this dark world and against the spiritual forces of evil in the heavenly realms." -Ephesians 6:12

Life is beset by conflict and troubles; even if you are divinely anointed, set apart and consecrated by God. It does not matter if you are rich or poor, a prisoner or a prophet, you can be sure that trials, troubles and tribulations will come your way. This is one thing we can all attest to, there are no exemptions from the troubles of this world.

"So as David stood there among his brothers, Samuel took the flask of olive oil and anointed David. And the Spirit of the LORD came powerfully upon David from that day on." -1 Samuel 16:13 NLT

David was anointed to be king early in life. David is known as the "man after God's own heart", but his own son Absalom wanted to kill him and tear his kingship apart. Although David had God's divine favor in every battle, giving him victory over all of his enemies, several years later he ran for his life from Saul. Then he faced the hardest temptation of life when he saw

Bathsheba, Uriah's wife and desired her. He eventually had to face his troubles. David later returned to rule Israel.

The scripture warns the world to, *"touch not my anointed ones and do my prophets no harm." 1Chronicles 16: 22*

No matter how heavy the load, or how deep the burdens of life weigh you down, the anointing will do the lifting and without any sacrifice!

We can all operate under God's anointing in this life. The only requirement is that we first believe in Jesus Christ and make the choice to live a righteous life. One key we must try to understand is that many problems in life serves a purpose. These difficulties test your resolve, your conviction, test your character and through it all strengthen your faith. It may be painful, but it is profitable to the soul.

Blessings to You!!!

Study Scriptures:

"The Lord is close to the brokenhearted; he rescues those whose spirits are crushed. The righteous person faces many troubles, but the Lord comes to the rescue each time." Psalms 34:18-19 (NLT)

"He heals the brokenhearted and bandages their wounds. He counts the stars and calls them all by name. How great is our Lord! His power is absolute! His understanding is beyond comprehension! The Lord supports the humble, but he brings the wicked down into the dust." Psalms 147:3-6 (NLT)

God Offers Comfort to All

All praise to God, the Father of our Lord Jesus Christ. God is our merciful Father and the source of all comfort. He comforts us in all our troubles so that we can comfort others. When they are troubled, we will be able to give them the same comfort God has given us. For the more we suffer for Christ, the more God

105

will shower us with his comfort through Christ. Even when we are weighed down with troubles, it is for your comfort and salvation! For when we ourselves are comforted, we will certainly comfort you. Then you can patiently endure the same things we suffer. We are confident that as you share in our sufferings, you will also share in the comfort God gives us. We think you ought to know, dear brothers and sisters, [a] about the trouble we went through in the province of Asia. We were crushed and overwhelmed beyond our ability to endure, and we thought we would never live through it.
 2 Cor. 1:3-8 (NLT)

"The most important thing in life is to stop saying 'I wish' and start saying 'I will.' Consider nothing impossible, then treat possibilities as probabilities."
Charles Dickens

Chapter Nine

EBENEZER STONE

Back in ancient times stones were used for multiple purposes. The most common stone was limestone and flint, formed from soil, clay and minerals. Wood was considered to be scarce. Houses, walls, temples, columns and streets were built from hewn stone. Stones because of its abundance was used as weapons against the enemy. The stones were thrown onto the opponent's fields to ruin their agriculture and stones were used to block wells in order to create drought and hydration in the camp. There were also more practical uses of stones. They were used for sacred and spiritual purposes. Memorials were built from large stone to mark graves and events. As you can see stone was used for more than just, capital punishment or stoning. Christ himself is known as the chief cornerstone, symbolizing the strength and foundation of our Christian faith.

The Ebenezer (stone of help) the name
of a place and moment in Israel's
history.

> 1. The place where Israel was
> attacked and defeat by the
> Philistines and the Ark of The
> Covenant was captured.

> 2. A stone erected by Samuel to
> commemorate Israel's victory
> over the Philistines. It may have
> been named Ebenezer to show
> that Israel's defeat there 20 years
> earlier had been reversed
> (1 Samuel 7:12)

Ebenezer means "stone of help." Every
time an Israelite saw the stone erected
by Samuel, it was a tangible reminder of
the Lord's power and protection. The
"stone of help" marked the spot where
the enemy had been defeated and God's
promise to bless His repentant people
had been honored. The Lord helped
them all the way to Ebenezer.

It shows how amazing our God is! The same enemy who defeated Israel twenty years earlier had to come back and face them again. But this time, Israel strengthened themselves in the Lord. They prayed and repented of past sins. When the enemy attacked the second time, with the Lord's help, they gained the victory. The lesson is very clear, whatever we try to handle without the help of the Lord will generally fail. But when we yield to God's plan, we will come out victorious and the enemy we will see no more.

There are times in life when we all feel defeated. Maybe because we tried to handle it and fight the battle on our own. If we consult with God first, repent and humble ourselves before Him, then we can endure the fight. Yielding to the divine plan of God will bring victory over the enemy in every area of life.

The enemy may attack, but with the help of God he cannot destroy. No weapon formed against you shall prosper. A great tip is to journal the trials and tribulations of your journey. Especially those times when you are under heavy attack. Take the biggest stone and name it Ebenezer, meaning this is the time that the Lord helped to bring me the victory.

Mark The Spot!

We should mark a spot or make a memorial of the places and times that God helped us and delivered us into victory. I think it is easier to remember the tough times or the rough spots in life, because Satan is always there to remind you of these not so good times. But on the flip side, it is a bit more challenging to remember all the good times and good the Lord has done in your life.

Both my mother and father have passed on from this earth. If I press my mind hard enough, I can recall specific dates and times. These were tough spots for me seeing them transition, as I am sure it is tough spots for most people. But I chose to mark and remember the good moments while they were present here on earth. I can easily recall the joy, the love, the discipline and direction they provided in my life. There are pictures of events, and special things from each of them that I hold dear to my heart.

We should set an Ebenezer stone in place to mark the spot in remembering the good things, and the victories over our enemy. Not a memorial to your own strength, not praising your goodness, but to honor and glorify God for his goodness. One of my close friends had a beautiful brick home built in Texas. During the pouring of the foundation, the couple opened the bible to their favorite scripture, covered the Bible in plastic and laid the Bible in the concrete of the foundation. What a great way to honor God! They set up their Ebenezer stone for many generations to come.

Another family friend when purchasing
their new home placed wooden
decorative crosses out front in the
flower beds as a sign of victory and
honor to God. Also, inside were
scriptures printed on the walls of the
stairways. In the center of my family
room is the scripture of Deuteronomy
28:6 in a large frame to welcome all
blessings coming and going.

When I was young growing up in
Alabama, just about every house I
visited had some kind of emblem with
scripture honoring God's goodness.
Sometimes there would be a bible on
the coffee table or pictures of scripture
hung on the walls. These were also used
as markings to anyone entering the
home that is God's House and bad
spirits are not welcome. Now that our
current society is largely driven by
technology, these ideals are rarely seen
in homes, but this should not change
our devotion of God's manifested
goodness.

What are you doing to set your Ebenezer stone? Has God delivered you through dangers seen and unseen, or brought you through when you thought there was no way out? Has He blessed you in any significant way that is worthy of recognizing and acknowledging his manifested goodness? If the answer is yes, then set your stone as a reminder and for the many generations to come.

Blessings to You!!!

Study Scriptures:

*Then Samuel said, "Gather all Israel to
Mizpah and I will pray to the Lord for
you." They gathered to Mizpah, and drew
water and poured it out before the Lord,
and fasted on that day and said there,
"We have sinned against the Lord." And
Samuel judged the sons of Israel at
Mizpah. Now when the Philistines heard
that the sons of Israel had gathered to
Mizpah, the lords of the Philistines went
up against Israel. And when the sons of
Israel heard it, they were afraid of the
Philistines. Then the sons of Israel said
to Samuel, "Do not cease to cry to the
Lord our God for us, that He may save us
from the hand of the Philistines." Samuel
took a suckling lamb and offered it for a
whole burnt offering to the Lord; and
Samuel cried to the Lord for Israel and
the Lord answered him. Now Samuel was
offering up the burnt offering, and the
Philistines drew near to battle against
Israel. But the Lord thundered with a
great [a]thunder on that day against the
Philistines and confused them, so that*

they were [b]routed before Israel. The men of Israel went out of Mizpah and pursued the Philistines, and struck them down as far as below Beth-car. Then Samuel took a stone and set it between Mizpah and Shen, and named it [c]Ebenezer, saying, "Thus far the Lord has helped us." -1Samuel 7:5-12 (NASB)

"You will not have to fight this battle. Take up your positions; stand firm and see the deliverance the LORD will give you, Judah and Jerusalem. Do not be afraid; do not be discouraged. Go out to face them tomorrow, and the LORD will be with you." 2 Chronicles 20: 15 NIV

Chapter Ten

STEPPING STONES

> *"Shall I pursue and will I over take them?"* The Lord responded, *"pursue and you will recover all."*

The Merriam Webster Dictionary defines stepping stone as something that helps to get or achieve something. The challenge for us all is to take the stones that are thrown at us and use them as building blocks for stepping higher. Whatever tough issues we deal with in life should not set us back, instead it should be used to set us up for something bigger and better. The hard things in life is the foundation needed for advancing your progress.

King David in 1Samuel 30, demonstrates a way to manage the hate and hurt when friends turn against you or should I say "threaten to stone you." David was accompanied by valiant men who he had been with through many battles. They were by most measure devoted friends and followers of David, and even deemed as close as brothers. They camped out in caves together while hiding from Sauls' threat to murder David and his men. One day after returning from battle, they found their camp at Ziglag raided and burned to the ground. All their wives and children along with their possessions were gone, taken captive. The men were so hurt and confused they suddenly began to blame David and threatened to stone him. But then a remarkable thing happened. David did not allow the negative words and acts of being stoned cause him to react to their hateful ideals. David also lost his wives and all of his possessions, chose to pray. He stole away and prayed to God about the situation. *"Shall I pursue and will I over take them?"* The Lord responded, *"pursue and you will recover all."*

The hearts of some of the men were softened and they put down the stones and followed David and recovered everything that had been stolen. In fact, they also gained the possessions of their enemies and shared the spoils of the battle with the men back at the camp who chose not to make to journey. David used the "threats of being stoned by his men," as stepping stones and did not allow the situation to become a stumbling block. We too should take David's example of placing God first before flesh first. Pray about it and seek God's guidance. His wisdom and guidance is always readily available to us simply by asking. He wants us to seek first His kingdom and his righteousness and we will find that His answers will be right and will be right on time for everything situation.

Don't allow what others say about you determine your destiny in life. No matter what stones are thrown your way, don't get distracted from pursuing your goals, your dreams or your purpose.

I recall many years ago as I started on my career path, I was challenged, slandered, labeled and even denied.

What surprised me was the ones who were throwing the stones. I am convinced that some of them didn't even know that the devil was using their words to batter my spirit, to deflate my confidence and zap my energy. There were all kinds of stones thrown my way. I know the enemy wanted to discourage me from pressing forward with the plans that God had purposed for me. I cried and sought advice from others I felt was in a higher position in life and maybe had gone through some of the same struggles, but they were preoccupied with current struggles. I was aggravated and frustrated because I knew there was something greater in me that I couldn't quite reach, and it seemed no one was willing to help me or give me a chance. But when I learned to cry out to God and cut away some of the dead weight and seek his purpose for me, my life changed for the better. I had no idea the pain of the process would make me better and stronger. Now, years later I can look back and appreciate the struggle and the process. It taught me a lot about myself, in terms of my faith in God, faith in my gifts, my toughness, determination and my commitment to reaching new heights in Christ. It strengthened my commitment to gain a better life for me and my family. I am determined to keep away the curse of failure for my family, friends and for this generation and many generations to come.

I thank God to this day for giving me strength, wisdom and the courage to take the stumbling blocks and make them stepping stones. So, I say to you whatever stones are being hurdled at you, take the negative intent of these stones and use them to build your foundation for success.

A Right Mindset!

Living a higher life in Christ is all about having the proper mindset. It is about having a mindset of faith, confidence and belief. Belief must be so deep that it permeates your entire being. When this happens, you have the spiritual power to ward off doubt and fear. Pushing back on the internal questioning and the battles that take place in your own mind.

You have to know who you are in Christ!

"They do not know, nor do they understand; They walk in darkness; All the foundations of the earth are unstable. I said, "You are gods, and all of you are children of the Most High." Psalms 82:5-6

You are gods! You see it written and spoken in scriptures. You have godly powers to infect and affect any environment. When you live from the power that is within, you can impact any situation for good. When you become comfortable in your own skin, you can walk in the peace, power and the presence of your kingship and queenship. "Spiritual Royalty."

When life throws you trials and tribulations, these should be seen as mire stepping stones in preparation for the greater things. Jesus being the Son of God was mentally tested by Satan, after forty days of fasting and praying. You should expect some intense testing to make sure you know who you are and whose you are. In order to be light in the world, you will have to experience walking in darkness. To live a life above, you must experience living beneath (without). There are some lessons you may not grip right away. But God will show you more and give you more when your faith and obedience is aligned with His.

Your mind has the power to infect and affect your environment!

Those who live according to the flesh have their minds set on what the flesh desires; but those who live in accordance with the Spirit have their minds set on what the Spirit desires. The mind governed by the flesh is death, but the mind governed by the Spirit is life and peace. The mind governed by the flesh is hostile to God; it does not submit to God's law, nor can it do so. Those who are in the realm of the flesh cannot please God. -Romans 8:5-8NIV

When the mind is right, life rightly aligns with God.

When the mind is right, ministries are right

When the mind is right, relationships are right

When the mind is right, finances are right

When we get our mind right, we get our lives right with God. But we can only get our minds right, when we are focused on the Spiritual things of God.

What do you have your mind set on? Is your mind set, for something good or something evil? Something carnal or something spiritual; Something earthly or something heavenly!

Scripture tells us, since we are in Christ Jesus, then we should *set our minds on things above, not on earthly things. Col. 3:2*

What we think about, will reproduce itself. In others words what we focus our thoughts on, is what is manifested in our lives.

This is much greater than just mind over matter, it is having the right mind set that gives you the power to dominate and take authority of anything that matters.

"I count him braver who conquers his own desires than him who conquers his enemies; for the hardest victory is the victory over self." -ARISTOLE

Blessings to You!!!

Study Scriptures:

"I have told you these things so that in Me you may have peace. In the world you will have tribulation. But be of good cheer. I have overcome the world." John 16:33

"And you shall love the LORD your God with all your heart, with all your soul, with all your mind, and with all your strength.' This is the first commandment. And the second, like it, is this: 'You shall love your neighbor as yourself.' There is no other commandment greater than these." Mark 12:30-31 NKJV

If a man say, I love God, and hateth his brother, he is a liar: for he that loveth not his brother whom he hath seen, how can he love God whom he hath not seen? And this commandment have we from him, That he who loveth God love his brother also. (1 John 4:20-21 KJV)

David Destroys the Amalekites

Three days later, when David and his men arrived home at their town of Ziklag, they found that the Amalekites had made a raid into the Negev and Ziklag; they had crushed Ziklag and burned it to the ground. They had carried off the women and children and everyone else but without killing anyone. When David and his men saw the ruins and realized what had happened to their families, they wept until they could weep no more. David's two wives, Ahinoam from Jezreel and Abigail, the widow of Nabal from Carmel, were among those captured. David was now in great danger because all his men were very bitter about losing their sons and daughters, and they began to talk of stoning him. But David found strength in the Lord his God.

Then he said to Abiathar the priest, "Bring me the ephod!" So Abiathar brought it. Then David asked the Lord, "Should I chase after this band of raiders? Will I catch them?"

And the Lord told him, "Yes, go after them. You will surely recover everything that was taken from you!"

Chapter Eleven

BURDEN OF UN-FORGIVENESS

Forgiveness means to release and let go of resentment in order to free yourself from the pain and the shame of the past and the present. This is not just about forgiving others, but much more about forgiving self. Yes, there are somethings we all have come short of in life. Although we are not where we should be, it is by the grace of God that we are not where we use to be.

Forgiveness is a conscious and moral choice, but more so a spiritual requirement! It is one of the spiritual gifts that we do not practice often enough. "Good practices doesn't make you perfect, but it does make you better. It is a must that we practice routinely the gift of forgiveness. By saying three words, "I forgive you," is a great start to the heartfelt gift of forgiveness.

My in-laws were married for 56 years when Mr. Harris departed into Heaven. They made a practice of kissing, praying, and asking each other for forgiveness for whatever they had said or done that was negative or hurtful to each other before bedtime every night. They never let the sun go down on their anger, just as the scripture speaks of in Ephesians 4:26. Their lives were far from perfect and Mrs. Harris would say they had a lot of years of practice to get things right. This practice of forgiveness kept their marriage healthy and happy. They did not give the enemy a way to creep in through the back door of un-forgiveness. If un-forgiveness is not of God, it must be a tactic of the Enemy!

> "Forgive others, not because they deserve forgiveness, but because you deserve peace."
> -Jonathan Lockwood Huie

Peter asked Jesus, *"Lord, how many times shall I forgive my brother when he sins against me?" "Up to seven times?"* Jesus answered, *"I tell you, not seven* times, but seventy-seven times." We are constantly asking God to forgive us, yet we are unwilling to walk in this practice of faith and forgive others!

King David pinned these words in Psalm 103:10-12, so that we today could see through his witnessing and through his life experiences the benefits and the unmeasurable love and forgiveness from God. *"He does not punish us for all our sins; nor does he deal harshly with us, as we deserve. As the heaven is high above the earth, so great is his mercy toward us. As far as the east is from the west, so has he removed our transgressions from us."*

Can you even envision this picture, as far as the east is from the west? That is a great distance in measurable space to describe how far God goes in forgiving our sins and separating our sins from us. Remembering them no more! So, stop hanging your head, and walking in the guilt of past sins. If you pray, repent whole heartily, ask God for forgiveness and believe, then God will forgive you.

"We must develop and maintain the capacity to forgive. He who is devoid of the power to forgive is devoid of the power to love. There is some good in the worst of us and some evil in the best of us. When we discover this, we are less prone to hate our enemies." -Martin Luther King, Jr.

Next, forgive yourself. There are things that happen in life that leaves indelible marks. Negative events will to shape us, mold us and make us into something we are not. It can leave you tainted with the feeling of guilt and the shame of un-forgiveness.

King David's life was full of drama. It was an emotional roller coaster, experiencing defeat after great victory. He engaged another man's wife and even took Uriah's life. But God in his infinite mercy forgave David. Today David is known for being "the man after God's own heart."

When life happens don't forget that God is a faithful, just, and a forgiving God. We only have to ask God whole heartedly and he will forgive our sins and restore our joy.

"Blessed is the man whose transgressions are forgiven, whose sins are covered, and whose sins the Lord does not count against him and in whose spirit is no deceit." -Psalms 32 1:2

If David the adulterer and murder was forgiven of his sin, this is a sign to world that God has a heart that is big enough to forgive you of all your sins. If Paul the chief murder and executer of the Saints of God was forgiven, just image how much more God is willing and able to forgive you.

Forgiveness is a part of God's nature. This was shown to the world when Jesus died on the cross for our sins. Now we can love each other, more importantly we can forgive others and ourselves. God knows our weakness and the dust from which we were formed. He forgives us of our sins and removed our sins. Likewise, there is cost that you must pay to receive God's forgiveness, you have to forgive others. We all have sinned and fallen short of the glory of God, so let us not be so quick to judge others when they sin or fall into temptation. You may not have committed the same sin as the next person, but sin of any kind is still sin.

Peter asked the question, *"Lord how often shall my brother who sin against me, and I forgive him, up to seven same times?" Jesus replied, I did not tell you up to seven times, but I say up to seventy times seven.*

This is a key principle of forgiveness; Forgive, as God has forgiven you...

I personally experienced the conviction of the Holy Spirit and had to go back and ask some people in my past to forgive me for hurtful things I had done and said. Many of those people were more than willing to grant me the forgiveness. For those who did not, it is no longer my burden but theirs. I am free from the burden of the past sins and God has released me to move on!

If you are carrying the weight associated with un-forgiveness, I urge you to "release it and let it go." It is not worth losing another night of sleep over. Just stop right now at this very moment, close your eyes and say, Lord I forgive and I release it, I am giving unforgiveness back to Satan. This burden is not meant for me to carry. In Jesus Name, I release it. Now take three deep breaths and slowly exhale and feel the relief!!!

Forgive even the unforgivable, as The Lord has forgiven you!

The weak can never forgive. Forgiveness is an attribute of the strong. - Mahatma Gandhi

The Domino Affect!

There are some sins in life that some people would prefer to keep hidden. Somehow hoping that if it is buried, it will go away or disappear.

But that is not the case, sin should be admitted and confessed, then we can ask God for forgiveness. This gives you the power to confront the enemy knowing there is no condemnation to the believer.

If we do not address our sins, it can cause damage to hit unintended targets. Your sin can trickle down to your family; to your children and your children's children until the sin has a strong hold on the entire family. We all have seen how sin can take control over a family. The mother and daughter have the same sin issue or the father and son have the same sin issue. The only way to defeat these actions is to confront it through truth and faith is God.

Although these sins may have started out small, the longer you take to repent, the stronger the issue gets to overpower you and possibly those connected to you. But God's plan is designed for you win in the end!

Blessings to You!!!

Study Scriptures:

"Bear with each other and forgive whatever grievances you may have against one another. Forgive as the Lord forgave you." Colossians 3:13 (NIV)

"He has not dealt with us after our sins nor rewarded us according to our iniquities. For as the heavens are high above the earth, so great are His mercy and loving-kindness toward those who reverently and worshipfully fear Him. As far as the east is from the west, so far has He removed our transgressions from us. As a father loves and pities his children, so the Lord loves and pities those who fear Him [with reverence, worship, and awe]." (Psalm 103:10-13 AMP)

"Brothers and sisters, if someone is caught in a sin, you who live by the Spirit should restore that person gently. But watch yourselves, or you also may be tempted. Carry each other's burdens, and in this way, you will fulfill the law of Christ." (Galatians 6:1-2 NIV)

"Let the wicked change their ways and banish the very thought of doing wrong. Let them turn to the LORD that he may have mercy on them. Yes, turn to our God, for he will forgive generously. "My thoughts are nothing like your thoughts," says the LORD. "And my ways are far beyond anything you could imagine. For just as the heavens are higher than the earth, so my ways are higher than your ways and my thoughts higher than your thoughts." (Isaiah 55:7-9 NLT).

"If we say we have no sin [refusing to admit that we are sinners], we delude ourselves and the truth is not in us. [His word does not live in our hearts.] If we [freely] admit that we have sinned and confess our sins, He is faithful and just [true to His own nature and promises], and will forgive our sins and cleanse us continually from all unrighteousness [our wrongdoing, everything not in conformity with His will and purpose]." 1John 1:8-9 (AMP)

Chapter Twelve

A DIVIDED HOUSE

There is nothing wrong with differences. In fact, God in His infinite wisdom created differences all over the universe. Differences are very evident in nature. If you look at the flowers and the trees; several different trees grow side by side in the same soil but it produces different fruit. If there is an appreciation for nature and its differences, there should be an appreciation for human beings and their differences.

The diversity of thought should be appreciated and not eliminated. Having multiple views should help render the best solution. There is a tendency around the world to punish, maim or kill people with different religious viewpoints. Jesus doesn't care about mans' religion. He wants our relationship.

America is acknowledged around the world as the land of opportunity and the place for people to pursue their hopes and dreams. It is recognized as the country where the more ambitious you are, the greater the reward. Although America is the best when it comes to democracy and freedoms it could still possibly destroy itself through mistrust and corruption. God's people should slow down and take more time to pray!

There exists a deep sense of divide in our culture that is hidden beneath the surface but often is chosen to be ignored. Pretending all is well and hoping that somehow it will all go away and heal itself. Just sprinkle some magic dust and poof the troubles are gone! And I must add, the same feelings of hatred and distain exist around the world. But we as followers of Christ are called be the unifying voice.

We cannot allow this hatred, racism and bigotry to win. Do not forget that underneath the skin we are all alike "one human race," and we all are kin in the Spirit realm. I know this matter goes much deeper than the color of your skin. We have to deal with truth, if not, the enemy will play the game of chance and he expects to win.

Just because;
Just because others don't look like you, doesn't mean that you should not learn to love them too. Just because they don't worship your way, it is all in God's hand, He teaches us all how to worship and how to pray!

> "Injustice anywhere is a threat to justice everywhere. We are caught in an inescapable network of mutuality, tied in a single garment of destiny. Whatever affects one directly, affects all indirectly."
> -Martin Luther King Jr.

"No one is born hating another person because of the color of their skin, or his

background, or his religion. People must learn to hate, and if they can learn to hate, they can be taught to love, for love comes more naturally to the human heart than its opposite."
-Nelson Mandela

"Hate is like an acid. It damages the vessel in which it is stored, and destroys the vessel on which it is poured." -Ann Landers

Let's look at what King David divinely pinned about being individually, and specially created by God.

"You made all the delicate, inner parts of my body and knit me together in my mother's womb. Thank you for making me so wonderfully complex. Your workmanship is marvelous—how well I know it." -Psalms 139:13-14 (NLT)

We all are fearfully and wonderfully created. We are equally gifted and anointed as "one "in Spirit. Yet, we've allowed the enemy to separate, divide and dilute our powers of unity and love.

Satan's strategy appears to be working. He causes division amongst God's people. But Jesus knowing men thoughts from afar said, *"Every kingdom divided against itself is brought to desolation; and every city or house divided against itself shall not stand."* Matthew 12:25

If you have ever witnessed a family fight it can be one of the most viscous and vile battles to witness. Whether it be husband against wife, mother against daughter, or a father against son, it is all ugly. It does not matter what is at the heart of the issue, it tears at the fiber of our existence and goes against "God's divine plan and purpose for the family."

I know God's divine purpose is for His people (all the people of the world) to live in unity. God in His infinite wisdom created such a diverse human race that He gave different yet, similar gifts in order that we might unite under the greatness of His glory. Our differences are not designed to divide us but rather unify. Hello world, wake up and see what the enemy is trying to do!

Any warfare is harmful and divisive no matter who is at fault or who is to blame. It is by the grace of God that any bad behavior has never happen to you in life. Just as God forgives us, we must continually practice the commandment of forgiveness with others. If we humble ourselves, repent and turn back to God, He has made provisions to forgive and bless us at levels of abundance that we have never experienced before.

"Now I beseech you, brethren, by the name of our Lord Jesus Christ, that ye all speak the same thing, and that there be no divisions among you; but that ye be perfectly joined together in the same mind and in the same judgment." (1 Corinthians 1:10 KJV)

If this world is to stand, we all must pull together "as one" and follow God's master plan!

"Let us not seek the Republican answer or the Democratic answer, but the right answer. Let us not seek to fix the blame for the past. Let us accept our responsibility for the future." John F. Kennedy

In House Fighting

There are conflicts in churches that cause spiritual separation, frustration and ministry devastation. There is clash over recognition and positions for worldly ambition causing us to lose sight of God's mission.

"I appeal to you, by the name of our Lord Jesus Christ, that all of you agree, with no divisions among you, but be united in the same mind and the same judgment." 1Corinthians 1:10

The enemy deceives by pitting saints against each other over small differences. These differences do not make either less than nor greater than the other, but only gives the false pretense that one is more superior.

There are different kinds of gifts, but the same Spirit distributes them. There are different kinds of service, but the same Lord. There are different kinds of working, but in all of them and in everyone is the same God at work. 1 Cor. 12:4-6

We fight each other for no reason. Those with higher levels of understanding have to act accordingly. We have authority over matters on earth. It is not for us to mirror the attitude of this world. A carnal mind will draw you away from the things of the kingdom.

The greater purpose and plan that God has for this life is worth fighting for. We all understand that life itself is a fight.

Whether it is keeping a roof over your head or a fight for health or just holding onto mental sanity.

In spite of these challenges, it is worth fighting for, there is so much more that God has in store.

Blessings to You!!!

Study Scriptures

A House Divided Cannot Stand

Then one was brought to Him who was demon-possessed, blind and mute; and He healed him, so that the blind and[a] mute man both spoke and saw. And all the multitudes were amazed and said, "Could this be the Son of David?"

Now when the Pharisees heard it they said, "This fellow does not cast out demons except by Beelzebub,[b] the ruler of the demons."

But Jesus knew their thoughts, and said to them: "Every kingdom divided against itself is brought to desolation, and every city or house divided against itself will not stand. If Satan casts out Satan, he is divided against himself. How then will his kingdom stand? And if I cast out demons by Beelzebub, by whom do your sons cast them out? Therefore, they shall be your judges. But if I cast out demons by the Spirit of God, surely the kingdom of God has come upon you. Matthew 12: 22-28 (NKJV)

Above all, love each other deeply, because love covers over a multitude of sins. -1Peter 4:8

If a man say, I love God, and hateth his brother, he is a liar: for he that loveth not his brother whom he hath seen, how can he love God whom he hath not seen? And this commandment have we from him, That he who loveth God love his brother also. -1 John 4:20-21 (KJV)

If my people, which are called by my name, shall humble themselves, and pray, and seek my face, and turn from their wicked ways; then will I hear from heaven, and will forgive their sin, and will heal their land. -Chronicles 7:14 (KJV)

Chapter Thirteen

BUT FOR GOD'S GRACE

We all have sinned and fallen short of the glory of God. If it had not been for the Lord on our side where would we be? None of us should feel so lofty that we put ourselves above anyone else, nor should we think of ourselves more highly than we ought to. We all have said things we should not have said and did things we should not have done. There are instances where we were the first to cast the stone, or the one who was quick to join in with the crowd as they piled on the stones against others. At one time or another we all have been a "stone thrower."

But God in his infinite wisdom has provided a way of escape. Glory be to God that we do not have to stay trapped in our past or current state of sin. "We are born into this world of sin, but by the grace of God we do not have to be stuck in a world of sin. We can simply ask God whole heartedly for his help. He is a just God who is willing to forgive. God's forgiveness will cover even the ones who threw stones and caused hurt.

There is even forgiveness for
bloodstained hands.

> *Let us then with confidence draw near to
> the throne of grace, that we may receive
> mercy and find grace to help in time of
> need.* -Hebrews 4:16

There is a lot to be said about God's
amazing Grace!
Mercian - Webster Dictionary shows a
varied degree of the definitions for the
word Grace.

1.   Unmerited divine
assistance given humans for their
regeneration or sanctification
2.   A virtue coming from God
3.   A state of sanctification
enjoyed through divine assistance

These three definitions are common
among multiple dictionaries. There are
many more definitive words we can use
to help us understand the goodness of
God's grace. Words such as favor,
mercy, pardon, privilege, reprieve and

exemption are all valid descriptions of God's Grace. I would also say that grace is God's continual display of his love for humanity. It is that agape or unconditional love. The kind of love that is given without expecting anything in return. This love (grace) is not something that is earned or deserved, but it is a divine gift, a spiritual flow of God's favor into the life of the believer.

Grace is:

A gift given when you do not deserve it.
A love offering when you did not earn it, and
A life sacrificed when you were not worthy of it.

We all have experienced some level of God's grace. The Holy Spirit ushers in Grace, (love, forgiveness and peace of God) when we least deserve it. When the world accuses us and courts say we are guilty, the Grace of God says we may be guilty; but all is forgiven.

We all witnessed scenes on Television or social media of people from different backgrounds, ethnicity and economic status, risking their lives to save people they did not know from the flood waters of Hurricane Harvey in Texas. This act was not the goodness of man alone, but the divine move of God on the hearts of man, a display of "God's Amazing Grace."

You may have experienced this grace when you applied for a job without having the proper qualifications. Or the time when you did not have the finances to send your kids to college, but then the school provided a full or partial scholarship. When the bills were due and the bank account was empty, but an unexpected check showed up in the mail box. These are just a couple of things that show up when we are operating under the Grace of God. But then there is a "greater grace," this is the level of grace that empowers us to minster to others in the power of the Holy Spirit in spite of our own issues and short comings. This great grace was spoken about in Acts 4 when Peter and John, filled with the Spirit, spoke with Holy Ghost boldness in addressing the Sanhedrin.

"This is the stone" which was rejected by you the builders, which has become the chief cornerstone. Nor is there salvation in any other, for there is no other name under heaven given among men by which we must be saved. And with great power the apostles gave witness to the resurrection of the Lord Jesus. And great grace was upon them all. -Acts 4:11-12, 33 NKJV

Grace is God's Goodness
Goodness is not a passive quality, but a deliberate alternative of right over wrong, a resistance of all moral evil to choose all moral good. It does not matter how good you think you are, remember God's manifested goodness is much greater. God can do exceedingly and abundantly more than we can ever ask or think. The goodness that you see

men display is a mere reflection of the goodness of the Holy Spirit that rests within the hearts of men. Not only is God good to us, but he demonstrates his love and grace through us.

Oh, taste and see that the Lord is good; Blessed is the man who trust in Him. (Psalm 34:8 KJV)

God wants the best for our lives and through the power of the Holy Spirit we can have the best and we can be the best.

Galatians 5:22 reminds us of that the fruit of the Spirit is *love, joy, peace, kindness, goodness, faithfulness, gentleness and self-control* which is granted to all who believe. I have seen these fruits manifested in my own life. The Holy Spirit has the power to mend broken pieces! He did it for Moses, turning him from a murderer to a minister. It was done for Paul turning from a persecutor to a preacher. Gideon was built up from a zero to a hero. God, the one who gives the Holy Spirit power to rebuild lives is still available today.

Grace is God's loving favor given to those seeking all the fruits of the Spirit. We cannot earn salvation, nor do we deserve it. No human efforts can gain it, because it comes only from God's mercy and His love. Without God's grace, we would not be saved. To receive it, we must acknowledge that we cannot save ourselves, He is the only way.

Blessings to You!!!

Study Scriptures:

But he gives us more grace. That is why Scripture says: "God opposes the proud but shows favor to the humble." James 4:6 (NIV)

Each of you should use whatever gift you have received to serve others, as faithful stewards of God's grace in its various forms. If anyone speaks, they should do so as one who speaks the very words of God. If anyone serves, they should do so with the strength God provides, so that in all things God may be praised through Jesus Christ. To him be the glory and the power for ever and ever. Amen. -1Peter 4:10-11 (NIV)

Three different times I begged the Lord to take it away. Each time he said, "My grace is all you need. My power works best in weakness." So now I am glad to boast about my weaknesses, so that the power of Christ can work through me. -2 Corinthians 12:8-9 (NLT)

But God, who is rich in mercy, for his great love wherewith he loved us, Even when we were dead in sins, hath quickened us together with Christ, (by grace ye are saved;) And hath raised us up together, and made us sit together in heavenly places in Christ Jesus: That in the ages to come he might shew the exceeding riches of his grace in his kindness toward us through Christ Jesus. For by grace are ye saved through faith; and that not of yourselves: it is the gift of God: Not of works, lest any man should boast.   -Ephesians 2:4-9 (KJV)

Keep your thoughts positive, because your thoughts become your words.

Keep your words positive because your words become your behaviors.

Keep your behavior positive because your behavior become your habits.

Keep your habits positive because your habits become your values.

Keep your values positive because your values become your destiny.
                    -Mahatma Gandhi

Closing Thought

Take the stones that are thrown at you and use them to build a foundation to a better life. Let now become your corner stone. What the devil meant for hurt, harm and evil, God will work it out for your good!

On these rocks build your own church, knowing that gates of hell cannot not prevail against them, for "all glory belongs to God." Take those little stones, the big stones and even the sharp stones and use them as stepping stones to take you higher. Everything else around may stumble and fall, but you will be built up in the Word of God and more knowledgeable of the troubles of this world. Have confidence in God and the He will protect you help you. You will not dash your foot against the stones of life.

Sometimes people throw stones at you intentionally and other times unintentionally. Either way, they can have the same harmful and hurtful impact. For those who walk under the favor and anointing of God will feel the same hurt from the stones being thrown. But now we will understand that we are more than conquerors and that no weapon formed against us will prosper if we keep our faith in God. We know the Lord will make our enemies our foot stool and the stones our stepping stones.

Stones are good for building a solid, firm and strong foundation!

As long as you keep a person down, some part of you has to be down there to hold him down, so it means you cannot soar as otherwise might. -Marian Anderson

Do not throw away the stones thrown at you. Use them to build your faith. They are stepping stones to your success!

Prayer Time

Our Father in Heaven, release us from the burden and the weight of un-forgiveness. Help us Lord to forgive others as you have forgiven us. Where there are signs of stubbornness, we humbly ask the Holy Spirit to guide us and not allow us to be hard hearted and miss our blessings therefore causing others to miss their blessings as well.

Heavenly Father, we ask that you forgive those who hurt us and those who might be hurting us right now, knowingly or unknowingly. Help us Jesus to handle the shame while dealing with the pain. Teach us Lord not to lean on our own understanding, due to evil things that may happen in life that we don't understand. Give us the mind and the heart to acknowledge you in all our ways and allow you to direct our path.

Strengthen us Lord, with courage and Godly integrity to do what is right at all times, regardless of the circumstances.

As we finger through your Word today in this book, we claim this day to be the day of breakthroughs. We claim and receive blessings through the words from this book. Help me Lord not to pile up or throw stones against my fellow man. Teach me to live and to love others as you love me. We thank you and we praise you. In Jesus Name Amen!

REFERENCES

Holy Bible, New King James Version
Copyright 2001 Holman Bible
Publisher, Nashville TN.

Life Application Study Bible, New
International Version, Zondervan NIV
Tyndall House Publisher, Inc. Wheaton,
Illinois and Zondervan Publishing
House Grand Rapids Michigan

biblegate.com online bible reference
search (NIV, NLT, NKJV, KJV)

The Essential Wisdom of the World's
Greatest Thinkers - Carol Kelly-Gang,
Fall Rivers Press, NY

Nelson's New Bible Dictionary
Copyright 1991,1986 by Thomas
Nelson Publishers

Clean House Strong House, Kimberly
Daniels Copyright 2003 by Kimberly
Daniels